"Not since Ralph Ellison's *Invisible Man* has any author captured so powerfully and authentically the essence of what life is like in America for African American men. Dr. Franklin diagnoses the many problems caused by callous, arrogant, and sometimes unintended actions with which African American men live every day of their lives. Dr. Franklin breaks new ground by prescribing spiritual and psychological steps that can be taken to overcome these problems. This book is a must read for clergy and all those in the helping professions who desire to help African American men break out of the prisons and dungeons of invisibility."

—*Dr. Jeremiah A. Wright, Senior Pastor, Trinity United Church of Christ, Chicago*

"Dr. Anderson Franklin travels to the core of Ralph Ellison's *Invisible Man* and reinterprets how this idea plays itself out today. For those African Americans who live with 'invisibility syndrome' daily and are in need of relief, he offers solutions. For a nation still oblivious to the ways it tears out the heart of our democratic republic, he offers a wake-up call."

—*Bakari Kitwana, author of* The Hip-Hop Generation: Young Blacks and the Crisis in African American Culture

"*From Brotherhood to Manhood* explores—with rich clinical wisdom—the unique burdens of being black and male in America. A. J. Franklin offers insightful advice to inspire men from any background. This forthright book should be read by everyone interested in understanding the obstacles along the journey toward manhood."

—*Alvin F. Poussaint, M.D., Professor of Psychiatry, Harvard Medical School*

"Dr. A. J. Franklin has been most generous to share decades of clinical experience in dealing with the problems black men in American society face. He has done significant analysis of the problems faced during all phases of life and shares them in interesting vignettes and scholarly presentations. I believe this can be an extraordinarily useful tool not only for black males, but for all of those who will be interacting with black males in American society."

—*Benjamin S. Carson, Sr., M.D., Director of Pediatric Neurosurgery; Professor of Neurological Surgery, Oncology, Plastic Surgery, and Pediatrics; Johns Hopkins Medical Institutions*

"Invisible brothers become visible men on the pages of this book. Dr. Franklin exposes the problem, unburdens the reader, gives hope for healing, and designs and forges new paths to visibility. What a debriefing!"

—*Dr. Gwendolyn Goldsby Grant, Psychologist, Advice Columnist,* Essence *magazine, and author of* The Best Kind of Loving

"This warm, real, and often heartbreaking book gives us an insider's view of what it is like to be black and male in this world. Dr. Franklin offers practical strategies for the affirmations needed and the celebrations required if we have men in our lives. If you know and care about a black man, you ought to read this book."

—*Gail E. Wyatt, Ph.D., Professor, Department of Psychiatry and Biobehavioral Sciences, UCLA Neuropsychiatric Institute; Director, Sexual Health Program; Associate Director, UCLA AIDS Institute; sex therapist; author of* Stolen Women *and coauthor of* No More Clueless Sex

From Brotherhood to Manhood

How Black Men Rescue Their Relationships and Dreams From the Invisibility Syndrome

Anderson J. Franklin, Ph.D.

WILEY

John Wiley & Sons, Inc.

Published by John Wiley & Sons, Inc., Hoboken, New Jersey
Published simultaneously in Canada

The author gratefully acknowledges the following for permission to quote from:
The Collected Poems of Langston Hughes by Langston Hughes, copyright © 1994 by the estate of Langston Hughes. Used by permission of Alfred A. Knopf, a division of Random House, Inc.
"The Frontier of Rage" by Askia M. Toure, by permission of the author.

For general information about our other products and services, please contact our Customer Care Department within the United States at (800) 762-2974, outside the United States at (317) 572-3993 or fax (317) 572-4002.

Wiley also publishes its books in a variety of electronic formats. Some content that appears in print may not be available in electronic books. For more information about Wiley products, visit our web site at www.wiley.com.

Library of Congress Cataloging-in-Publication Data:
Franklin, Anderson J.
   From brotherhood to manhood : how black men rescue their relationships and dreams from the invisibility syndrome / Anderson J. Franklin
      p. cm.
Includes index.
   ISBN 0-471-35294-2 (cloth)
 1. African American men. I. Title.
   E185.86 .F678 2002
   305.38'896073—dc21   2002014434
Printed in the United States of America

10 9 8 7 6 5 4 3 2 1

This book is dedicated to my parents:
Rev. Dr. Claude L. Franklin, Sr. and Mabel B. Franklin
and
to my uncles and cousin:
Irvin A. Franklin, Thomas A. Franklin, and Cleveland Jackson

ACKNOWLEDGMENTS

Writing this book is a story by itself. It is the result of many years of struggle on my part to illuminate the psychological journey of men of African descent for anyone who seriously wants to know what being black and male is all about. My persistence I can attribute only to a belief that this is a work for God. Finishing this book is the result of many people encouraging me along the way. To everyone who has supported me, I say thank you. There are those to whom I have a special indebtedness.

To my wife, Nancy, I am forever grateful for partnership, love, and optimism. She always had an unwavering belief that this book would be no less than a monumental success and refused to let me believe anything otherwise. Her own expertise and stature as a family psychologist was invaluable. She provided feedback and support on every draft of the manuscript. Moreover, in our many professional presentations together, her embrace of my ideas and constant promotion of them throughout her own professional engagements helped nurture this enterprise. I am truly blessed, and give all my love for her love.

Bringing this book to reality could not have happened without my agent, Marie Brown. She was a believer in its contribution and worked to position its acceptance by a publisher. I am indebted to my union with a talented and dedicated writer, Elza Dinwiddie-Boyd. Elza helped guide me through numerous rewrites of the manuscript, providing insights on writing for the general public as well as editing. Moreover, with her husband, Herb Boyd, another gifted writer, they freely shared their vast knowledge of history and richly informed insights on people of African descent. Their experiences as authors and learned perspectives on the African diaspora were a gift to this project, and the friendship that evolved from working together has blessed me with a new family.

Getting this book into final publication could not have happened without the foresight, support, and brilliance of my editor, Carole Hall at John Wiley and Sons. She is tried and true in support of this project, giving exceptional time and dedication to its creation. Her belief in its contribution has been steadfast, validating, and empowering. I am especially thankful for her talents and what has become a special friendship. At Wiley, I also thank Lisa Considine, Tom Miller, and Kim Nir.

I am also very thankful for my children, Deidre, Tunde, Remi, and Jay, who put up with the "old man's" preoccupation with writing and occasional unavailability. They sometimes became captive to my thinking aloud and offered insights from their generation on some of the issues discussed in the book.

Without my family I would not have taken on this writing journey or endured the roller-coaster ride of authorship. I was blessed to have grown up around my father, his brothers, and minister friends who gave me the foundation for my understanding of how to face challenges as a man of African descent. My mother, with her own indomitable strength and determination—always displayed with dignity, poise, and graciousness—provided balance to the male presence around the house. Moreover, as a trained teacher she was my first editor of many school papers, and she encouraged me to write.

My father, and my uncles Tommy and Irvin, and especially my cousin Cleveland were master storytellers in true Mississippi tradition. Any storytelling ability in these pages I attribute to them. It's my brother Claude, however, who is genuinely the keeper of this legacy. He has kept me laughing and attuned to this family tradition with his jokes and stories over the years. He has been my rock and best friend. I can always count on him being there for me.

There are of course my three childhood buddies, best friends, and brothers in the true sense of the word, Dr. Vernon Allwood, Dr. Randolf Tobias, and Dr. Thomas Turner. The journey down life's paths with Randy, Thom, and Vernon is indescribable and immeasurable in its meaning and worth to me. Together, over the years, we have confronted life, lived life, attempted to solve life's problems, particularly for people of African descent, with undiminished idealism, it seems, forever. Our life stories and experiences are essential to my understanding of men of African descent and my view on solutions. They each read, commented, and provided feedback on drafts of this manuscript. They also provided that necessary encouragement and always-needed digressions into laughter and fun. That spirit bonds us together, lifts my spirits, and is essential to my putting life into perspective.

Finally, thanks to some of the early believers that this work had potential, including Becky McGovern, Shirley Poole, Cheryl Greene, and Kay Clanton. It takes special people to work through very early versions of manuscripts and nurture someone's ideas. There were many colleagues who also gave me a chance to just chat, dialogue, present, and write about my insights on the invisibility syndrome for black men. They frequently inquired about my progress and gave encouragement. Thanks to Reginald Jones, James Jackson, Joseph White, James Jones, Robert Carter, A. Wade Boykin, Thomas Parham, Harriette and John McAdoo, and Algea Harrison, William Cross, and my student, Yasser Payne.

Special thanks go to Richard Simon of the Family Therapy Networker and Monica McGoldrick of the New Jersey Family Institute, who remain supporters and friends. It was at one of the annual Family Therapy Networker conferences that I had the privilege to hear and privately speak with Maya Angelou about an early draft of this manuscript and my scholarly ideas. Unbeknownst to her, by that brief conversation, she solidified my decision to make this work more accessible to the general public. Through sharing her own episodes with invisibility, as unbelievable as that seemed to me, along with her urging that scholar-practitioners like myself must do more to speak to the general public with our wisdom, I finally shifted the focus of my audience. I am grateful for the privilege to talk with her and for her encouragement.

AUTHOR'S NOTE

This book would not exist without the many men who have consulted me professionally. Their willingness to dare to be different in choosing individual or group counseling, or therapy—as a path to learning how to be a better man and person—has my utmost respect and gratitude. Their anonymity has of course been preserved in this book. Their inspiration, confidence, and trust in my ability to represent other truths about being black, of African descent, and male is an awesome responsibility that I take with great humility. However, any similarity of names or stories to known individuals is purely coincidental.

CONTENTS

PART FOUR

Moving On: From Brotherhood to Manhood   169

PREFACE

For over twenty years black men have opened their public and private lives to me. In support groups, in my private practice as a consultant and psychotherapist, and in my role as a professor and supervisor of clinical psychologists, different men call me their therapist, counselor, brother, or leader, because nobody knows them like I do—not even their mothers, wives, best friends, colleagues, or lovers. Giving me access to closely guarded inner worlds, my clients hope that somehow, through my profession, I can help them break through the invisibility of being black and male in America.

A sense of invisibility has become a commonplace experience, regardless of a person's race or gender. The hero of Ralph Ellison's novel *Invisible Man* epitomized this basic truth about the forces that complicate the search for identity in modern times. For black men today, the search is more confusing than ever, with untold consequences for our daily lives, families, and society. Every black male whose power and self-respect are real—and not a pose—recognizes the danger implicit in invisibility, understands the psychological pressure, and knows how to deal with it.

This book demystifies the way these effective men resist invisibility. I show how conscious and unconscious attitudes formed through years of invisibility can be reversed and channeled into personal fulfillment for black men as fathers, friends, workers, and partners to our women. *From Brotherhood to Manhood* teaches the following important skills:

- Spotting the subtle ways in which invisibility attacks our sense of personal power;
- Recognizing crises of invisibility—and what to do about them;

- Overcoming invisibility—how to counter the symptoms and lead the lives we envision.

I want to give more black men the tools to achieve the recognition, respect, inner peace, and integrity every healthy person seeks and many black men have already achieved. I am a firm believer that if you understand a problem you can solve it, instead of being immobilized by it. The good news, as I tell my clients, is that you can learn the skills to build your life according to your dream blueprints.

Throughout this book, I tell the true stories of men who turned to me for help. Some were friends who talked to me freely, knowing that, as a professional, I would respect the boundaries of confidentiality. Most were men who sought me out at the suggestion of loved ones who told them that they needed to talk to somebody about things that troubled them—managing anger, problems with careers and grievances in the workplace, broken relationships, depression, addictions, or crises of confidence.

Once a week for almost five years, some of the men whose stories you are about to hear came together in a closely knit support group. I provided a safe environment where they could break their silence and express their genuine problems about race and color—not just their BS. They could expose their feelings of hurt, indignation, anger, self-doubt, and even rejection of self. Over time they learned to trust and care about each other.

Outside the group, like most black men, they hid their full personalities behind various cool masks designed to protect them from the outside world. If people only saw the masks and were hostile or indifferent, at least no one could say that his genuine self had been rejected. But inside the group, often laughing and slapping low-fives in recognition of being friends and brothers, the men relaxed and traded stories.

It came as no surprise to me that their stories revealed an obsession with racial issues and injustices. Gender stereotypes and conventional assumptions about black men permeated their life experiences. Feelings of wanting to strike back and get even warred constantly with the men's motivation to excel and be accepted.

Ray, a corporate executive, could not shake off the memory of a day at the Harvard Club when he and his friend, a noted musical artist, were mistaken for doormen.

Jamal often referred to hiding the fact that he was a physician. He was certain that "sisters and brothers are always suspicious of my commitment," and if they knew about his professional life they would not treat him as a regular brother.

Treat—he acquired his nickname from his reputation for being able to sweet talk women into anything—opted out of the struggle to excel. He neglected his brilliance as a teacher and writer, hanging with friends in his old neighborhood, drinking, womanizing, and doing "a little" drugs.

"I have it under control, Doc," he often said.

Bill, a senior manager in a large New York firm, constantly raged against his parents, wife, son, and daughter, saying they did not understand the pressure he was under as one of few non-whites at his level in the company. In the group he was frequently the focus of attention, as the other men questioned his life decisions. Why wasn't he happy, given his high-paying career and model family? Why was he so angry, despite his successes? The men wanted answers for themselves as much as they did for Bill.

This book provides the answers and antidotes I know black men are looking for. Moreover, it provides the insight and information that others are missing when they try to help us.

On a recent morning, a racially mixed but mostly white audience of over three hundred doctors and nurses, ministers, mental health workers, psychologists, psychiatrists, and lay professionals attended one of my all-day workshops called "Overcoming Invisibility: Working Effectively with African American Men." As I travel around the world presenting workshops and attending conferences, I have witnessed a growing concern about the future of African American men.

Many people honestly want to encourage, support, or love us. But our wives, parents, sons and daughters, coworkers, counselors, teachers, youth workers, and others need a much better understanding of what it means to us to be black and male in this country to connect in any lasting way.

Millions of personal observations and reactions form a sounding board against which I bounce my interpretations of the African American male experience. As a result, the book also reflects the major passages and lessons of my own life as a son growing up in a black family with many strong male role models.

My late father, my extended family, and the males in my childhood neighborhood and church profoundly shaped my life and this work. So, too, did the dignity and counsel of many gifted black women in my family and role models of both genders at Virginia Union University and Howard University.

My father wanted me to follow him into the ministry. I know that he often smiles approvingly upon me from above. He got his wish. His resisting son ministers to the dreams—he would say souls—of black men.

PART ONE

THE ANATOMY OF INVISIBILITY

I am an invisible man. No, I am not a spook like those who haunted Edgar Allan Poe; nor am I one of your Hollywood movie ectoplasms. I am a man of substance, of flesh and bone, fiber and liquids—and I might even be said to possess a mind. I am invisible, understand, simply because people refuse to see me. . . . When they approach me they see only my surroundings, themselves, or figments of their imagination—indeed, everything and anything except me.

—Ralph Ellison, *Invisible Man*

1

INVISIBLE MEN

The Sixth Sense—Bill's Story

At forty-seven, Bill was part of the promising wave of poor-but-working-class black men who had made it into the middle class. Well-spoken and self-assured, he graduated from Yale in the late 1960s, served as an Army officer in Vietnam, and worked his way up the corporate ladder to a highly paid management position in a major American corporation.

He first came to see me because his son was having trouble in school, but it quickly became obvious that his son was having trouble with Bill. In fact, he was giving his whole family a hard time. He ranted at his son and daughter when they fought, minimized their conflicts, and told them to solve their problems on their own. He and his wife had grown increasingly distant, and the atmosphere at home was charged with tension and stress. He frequently came home from work withdrawn and impatient. Whenever he talked to his wife about his difficulties on the job, he told her angrily that she made him feel worse, misunderstood, and unsupported.

After about five weeks of family therapy a breakthrough occurred. During our session Bill revealed a disturbing incident, one that had unleashed an emotional firestorm. The night before, he had taken a white business client to an expensive restaurant in midtown Manhattan. When Bill told the maître d' they were there for dinner, the man looked right past him and asked his guest whether they had reservations. When the meal was over the waiter picked up Bill's American Express Gold Card, but then returned it with the charge slip to Bill's client.

Bill imagined how his father, a tough city bus driver who never let such racial slights go by, would have exploded at the waiter. But Bill, fearful of creating an embarrassing scene, simply reached over and signed the slip while continuing to chat amiably with his client.

The two men walked out into the night and shook hands, reaffirming their agreement on a major contract. It should have been a sweet moment: The agreement put Bill in line for a major promotion. The white client stepped to the curb and effortlessly hailed a cab. Fifteen minutes later Bill was still at the curbside with his hand up, while white men and women flowed around him to hail cabs of their own. Finally, after yet another cab passed him up in favor of a white couple, Bill flung himself across the hood, swearing and flailing his attaché case at the driver's window.

All evening he had struggled to contain his anger. He felt that he was being seen not as himself but as a stereotype—first, as too insignificant to host a client at an expensive restaurant, and then as too dangerous to be let into a cab. Later, he felt that his explosion of rage merely reinforced the stereotypes of menace, only further contributing to his invisibility.

Invisibility Defined

This was hardly the first time that an African American man in therapy had told me of race-related indignities. I believe that every black man, if you ask him, can describe comparable experiences in the pit of racism that happened either to him or to someone in his circle of family and friends. These experiences accumulate to create a feeling of invisibility.

Invisibility is an inner struggle with feeling that one's talents, abilities, personality, and worth are not valued or recognized because of prejudice and racism. Conversely, we feel visible when our true talents, abilities, personality, and worth are respected.

Obviously, Bill was not literally invisible. But being seen not as himself, and what's more, as utterly insignificant, infuriated him.

As I suspected, Bill's parents and relatives had made a point of teaching him from childhood how to detect and deal with racism. His older brothers and sisters threw in their opinions based on their experiences. Friends freely gave their personal guidelines based on what they learned through their own life experiences. Usually, with all of this input to draw on, Bill was able to navigate the hidden minefield of racism in the workplace. He had developed an invulnerability of sorts—an internal sense of being powerful enough to anticipate negative racial experiences, protect himself if necessary, and control his responses. But instead of protecting his dignity that night, his sixth sense had failed, and failing ignited a firestorm.

Most African American men understand what Bill went through. Daily acts of scorn are such a part of our experience that, early on, we develop a sixth sense or gut level sensor to detect contempt, slight, and innuendo in our encounters with other people. Invisibility is burdensome to black men's souls because it implies that we have been tricked, deceived, or compromised into humiliation, disgrace, or victimization. Feeling invisible, we have no dignity, and preserving our dignity is paramount.

Unfortunately, the effect of invisibility is that it links our self-respect to our ability to "read" (that is, to figure out) other people's intentions so that we can properly handle any racial situation we find ourselves in. Any shortcoming must be hidden behind a mask of indifference. The alternative is not much better: to fight aggressively to preserve what we think of ourselves. Either way, if you are an invisible man, to use novelist Ralph Ellison's timeless phrase, protecting your self-respect is a full-time job. It requires vigilance at all times, being careful in the evaluation of opportunities, and being assertive about personal goals in spite of what others think.

But all that effort can leave us at even greater risk, cool on the surface but underneath, lonely and confused. The following stories— indeed, the most common I hear from my clients—illustrate the dilemmas that are the outcome of risk to our formative selves.

Confused about How to "Be"—Tee's Dilemma

Tee, a dark-skinned ninth grader, could have been any black mother's son. He was obviously a bright kid. For years he repeatedly told teachers he wanted more instruction and homework in his favorite subjects. But almost every time he expressed his interest in math and science he got a quizzical look from his teachers. They would respond with insinuations about how difficult the subject was and how much he would have to study.

Since he stood six-four, his teachers instead encouraged him to play basketball. He liked the game. It was fun, but he was not interested in competing on a school team. He continued to surprise teachers with his membership in the science and math club even though he became re-signed to their attitudes. Tee and his mother had been waging this war against having his interests subverted since he started school. From independent testing they knew his intelligence and talents were exceptional. Nevertheless, he believed his teachers treated him as "the dumb black kid," or "jock."

Buttressed by his mother's support, Tee persisted in his academic interests, although he frequently felt like an oddball around his teachers. Among his black peers he was called a "brainiac," and was accused of trying to act white by being smart. He felt out of place and had to work hard to fit in on his terms. Except for his mother, he found few supporters.

Tee was not socially isolated. On the contrary, he was well-liked, and part of the school's social network. To accomplish this acceptance, however, he gradually learned to suppress his talents. In order to not appear to be such an oddity, he hung out with the "brothers," tried to "stay loose," and performed in class in a way that didn't overwhelm his teachers with his ability.

Tee was finding that he had to decide over and over again how he was going to be. His mother's, friends', and teachers' opinions and beliefs put a lot of pressure on him.

"Black boys get treated differently," his mother warned him. This was true. Or at least he began to feel that way. He could sense there was some truth in her passion, although her overprotective behavior embarrassed him when she thought the treatment he received was unfair and racially motivated.

As Tee struggled to craft a definition of himself that rose above the presumptions of people who had a real measure of control over him, he experienced an acute sense of invisibility. Boys like Tee find their way through the day with a sheer veil covering their eyes. They can see, but not with clarity. One moment they believe that they're headed in the right direction, and the next moment they're not so certain. People they rely on turn out to offer ambiguous and misleading cues about their strengths and direction.

Young black males who are less fortunate and supported than Tee can feel even more disoriented, exhausted at an early age by the effort it takes just to try to be accepted on their own terms. Take Carl for example, a twenty-six-year-old student government leader attending a well-known college.

Damned If You Do, Damned If You Don't—
Carl's Dilemma

After struggling through high school, Carl reluctantly earned his GED in an alternative public school program. He bounced from low-paying job to low-paying job and quickly became dissatisfied. Many of his friends were either headed to or just getting out of jail.

Sensing that Carl was drifting, his grandfather, a former navy man, urged him to join. Initially Carl resisted; but suddenly he relented and bought into his grandfather's sales pitch that it was an opportunity to see the world. What is more, Carl felt the uniform would give him recognition and a feeling of importance. But he thought little about how life would be in the navy.

Months after he joined, he found himself at sea with a group of young sailors whose acceptance of him was inconsistent at best. He frequently found himself excluded from social activities. All of the officers were white, and the few sailors of color blew hot and cold in their desire to have exclusive black friendships. Those black sailors who socialized only with each other were viewed, sometimes suspiciously, as different and loners. At times he felt accepted by them, and at other times they were suspicious of what was seen as his unusual friendliness with some white sailors.

Carl's grandfather had urged him to expand his horizons beyond his blackness, so he was not sure how he should act. Consequently, he would become whatever the people he was with wanted him to be at the time. As far as making friends and getting along with his fellow sailors, he felt as if he kept stubbing his toe as he tried to get along with different groups and follow the navy "team" credo—all while trying to be true to his grandfather's vision for him.

Carl tried hard not to allow the assumptions others held about him to overly affect the way he behaved. Ironically, his behavior helped reaffirm the opinions others held about him. This is the old "damned if you do, damned if you don't" dilemma. Trying to reconcile too many warring views created confusion and frustration, derailing his aspirations.

Wondering, *Why Bother?*—Kofi's Dilemma

"Hi, I'm Chris, but my friends call me Kofi." The handsome young man entered my office and extended his hand in greeting. He went on to say he was twenty-eight years old and that he felt that his life was drifting nowhere in particular. He wanted help getting back into school.

Kofi knew his parents wanted him to be proud of his heritage and make something of himself. Until he entered high school, Kofi attended a small private school run by an African American educator, where he was immersed in African and African American history as part of his basic education. He identified the transition to high school as one of the most difficult periods in his life.

His conflict began when he listened to a high school teacher talk about Dr. Martin Luther King Jr.'s winning of the Nobel Peace Prize and having a national holiday designated for him. In Kofi's view, the teacher related nothing of substance about the civil rights struggle central to Dr. King's accomplishments. Soon the depth of Kofi's understanding of African American history brought him into conflict with his teachers, who grew annoyed with his objections and challenges to their points of view. His parents supported this speaking up, which inevitably got him labeled as a difficult, albeit promising, student.

In standing up for values that were emphasized at home, Kofi had to deal with teachers who he felt disregarded those values. This was a dilemma throughout high school that twisted, rather than shaped his feelings about himself. He did not like being trapped between the two views of the world that he experienced at home and at school. Kofi felt his parents' "pushing me to have this black consciousness" became too frustrating. It got him in trouble at school where he was labeled a troublemaker. His parents, his teachers, and his minister all had divergent ideas about how he should behave, and his response to the conflicting cues was a resounding "Why bother?" By the time Kofi reached college, the pattern was set. Full of frustration, he dropped out in his second year.

Invisibility obscures personal vision. Assumptions and stereotypes that come from inside *and* outside our communities made it difficult for Kofi to achieve a balanced perspective on being black and male. Struggling constantly to maintain his self-esteem, he sought activities and alliances that allowed him to coexist with others, with the least amount of stress and with the maximum amount of dignity.

When you see a black man making choices or taking risks that aren't necessarily in his best interest, you can be fairly sure that those actions are making him feel valued above what others around him presume to be the small measure of his worth.

In Kofi, a sense of invisibility clouded his judgment and altered his ability to evaluate his stature and movement toward personal goals. Invisibility created a heightened sensitivity to indignities. It led to his questioning his own judgment about how others treated him, about how he fit into situations, and about how to conduct himself.

Second-Guessing—Sean's Dilemma

Persistent second-guessing sucks hope out of the air, undermines the will, and breaks the spirit. Sean, a thirty-six-year-old attorney, recently told me that even within the black community he is constantly on guard about other people's reactions to him. What, he wondered aloud, will the sisters he meets think and feel about him? What will other brothers think and feel? He also wondered how he will be treated outside the black community. Will he be accepted? What impression is he making? He feels that his survival is threatened by his inability to correctly read hidden messages coded into each encounter.

It is all too easy for men like Sean to feel like victims of society, rather than vital, contributing members of it. If persistent self-doubt destroys their personal vision, they can gradually become nobodies instead of somebody.

The Invisibility Syndrome—Signs and Symptoms of Living Under Siege

Bill, Tee, Carl, Kofi, and Sean are examples of a phenomenon that Dr. Chester Pierce, an African American psychiatrist with a distinguished career at Harvard University, calls *micro-aggressions*. I explained micro-aggressions in an article I wrote for the January 2000 *American Journal of Orthopsychiatry*. They are subtle acts or attitudes that are experienced as hostile, and that fit a history and pattern of personal racial slights and disregard. They act as status reminders by their implicit suggestion of our unworthiness. They convey a "Stay in your place" message.

A life history of micro-aggressions would make anyone extremely vigilant about personal dignity and self-respect. As these stories show, perpetual vigilance is stressful and tips some men toward counterproductive and dysfunctional behavior. Experiences of invisibility—i.e., the micro-aggressions or slights—are like viruses in the atmosphere. As a psychologist to black men, I'm alert for the symptoms. The more of them I see in a client, the greater is the likelihood that the virus of invisibility has already worked its way into his relationships and dreams, and that what started out like a cold has turned into pneumonia.

I've seen invisibility affecting black men in a variety of ways. The signs and symptoms that can begin to pile up include:

- Frustration
- Increased awareness of perceived slights

- Chronic indignation
- Pervasive discontent and disgruntlement
- Anger
- Immobilization or increasing inability to get things done
- Questioning one's worthiness
- Disillusionment and confusion
- Feeling trapped
- Conflicted racial identity
- Internalized rage
- Depression
- Substance abuse
- Loss of hope

The invisibility syndrome—the term I coined for this cluster of debilitating symptoms originating from profound reactions to perceived racial slights—limits the effective utilization of personal resources, the achievement of individual goals, the establishment of positive relationships, the satisfaction of family interactions, and the potential for life satisfaction.

In short, the invisibility syndrome consists of ever-increasing behavior, feelings, and thoughts that reduce your ability to accomplish goals, to form positive relationships with important people in your life, to be happy, and to fulfill your dreams.

Men experiencing the invisibility syndrome live as if they were under siege. They have a hard time distinguishing racial slights from other kinds of problems. Whenever their judgment is brought into question, they shut down emotionally. As a result, they lose their capacity for intimacy with family and friends. They feel even more embattled and guarded in the workplace. But they won't admit it.

The Progression of Symptoms: Falling Deeper into Invisibility

This book explores the sources, unfinished business, and ongoing tension underlying these symptoms. It also shows how they progress, if they are left unchecked.

Stage One: Frustration

During childhood we start to respond to the annoying conventional wisdom about how tough life is if you're black and male. To a child, these innocuous warnings are frustrating parental rules. But the invisibility syndrome starts with confusion, then self-doubting in association with racial identity and gender, because at an age when praise and approval from parents and others is crucial to positive identity formation, we learn that our behavior as a black boy disturbs other people and we must beware. We instinctively gear up to reduce these frustrations by creating our own rules for making it in the world. These early behaviors form the origin of our "brotherhood rules," our standards for respect.

Stage Two: Uncertainty

By adolescence we may become sensitive to slights and quick to get upset. A teen who is vulnerable to invisibility will have a chip on his shoulder. He will try to be cool, but have difficulty manipulating the way he wants to be seen as a man as he struggles with the realities of two dominant worlds in his life, black and white. He will attempt to conceal his inner nature, and harden his stance.

As the risks to our welfare increase, our mothers, preoccupied about our safety, reduce attention to teaching us adult responsibilities. Our parents' narrow focus in raising black boys to manhood (sometimes spoken of as "love our sons, raise our daughters") is at the expense of learning in a benign environment, where, for example, the values of attachment and commitment would develop more freely if they were linked to intimacy more than to safeguarding survival. Thus our personal safety dominates our concerns, attachments, and commitments as we stride toward manhood.

Stage Three: Conflict

Young men who are struggling with invisibility play with various identities, casting about for the proper one that works for them. They usually drink to lessen their pain and gain relief, self-medicating their uncertainty.

Some delve into other risky self-assuring behaviors. Some men will move on to greater substance abuse. Others may seek resolution through chameleonlike behavior, a person with many different public faces.

Passionate avoidance of being associated with stereotypes can result in our ignoring genuine needs. Many young black men will not ask for help in school, because it is assumed that such requests validate unflattering beliefs about our intelligence or the worth of men of African descent in general. What we are unable to do academically we do socially, developing our ability to chill, party, and "talk to the ladies." Having "fine mamas" by our side gives us recognition and creates a comfort zone in the company of other men, and temporarily quells inner demons.

Stage Four: Denial and Guilt

As invisibility becomes a theme in our lives, so does denial and guilt as we wrestle with our indignation. With a rising sense of helplessness, we sabotage relationships, avoid commitments, and deny responsibilities. We keep invisibility at bay by reducing our exposure to unfamiliar challenges and the company of people different from ourselves. Living perpetually behind a mask of bravado or indifference, we compromise our personal power, while privately battling micro-aggressions, real or imagined.

Personal Power: The Key to Surviving Invisibility

What is personal power, and how does it mitigate invisibility?

Seven important elements add up to a sense of personal power. Internalized, they enable us to remain grounded, no matter what's happening to us:

1. **Recognition**
2. **Satisfaction**
3. **Legitimacy**
4. **Validation**

5. **Respect**
6. **Dignity**
7. **Identity**

It's a reasonable assumption that compromising these elements subverts our attempts to be the kind of men we want to be. A closer look at this assumption reveals the fundamental road blocks to our emotional health.

Recognition: The Power of Feeling You Are Being Acknowledged by Others

Kevin walked into his first meeting as a union representative and surveyed the room, only to see that he was just one of a handful of people of color. As he made his way into the room, threading through the crowd, no one approached him or gave him any sign of recognition. He found himself automatically moving in the direction of a black person talking to someone on the other side of the room.

"Hi, is this your first meeting?" Kevin was relieved to hear the voice.

He turned and saw that the person was addressing another representative walking just behind.

"Okay! I'll wait and see if he greets me," Kevin thought. But the man didn't. In fact he escorted this new representative toward others for introductions. Kevin knew it would be a long night.

Whereas we might attribute Kevin's experience to a variety of benign reasons, it fit a historical category of racial encounters that made him wonder about how genuinely he was accepted wherever he went— and that also included how family members recognized and treated him at home.

Recognition is essential for feeling acknowledged. Its absence forced Kevin to look for other places that would provide it. If he didn't feel acknowledged or appreciated at home, he would look outside the home. If he didn't feel acknowledged in his community, he would establish linkages outside the community. If a child were like Kevin and didn't feel that teachers gave him sufficient recognition in class, he would look to fellow students in or out of class to provide the recognition.

If we don't find something in the workplace that fulfills our need for recognition, either we do our work grudgingly or we leave. Recognition can come in the form of simply being warmly welcomed at a business reception, or it can mean being recognized as employee of the month.

One way or another, we will get the amount of recognition we desire. It is a fundamental need. If we don't feel sufficiently recognized as professionals, we go out and start our own professional organizations. If we do not feel welcome in local establishments, we create our own hangouts in innumerable places—barbershops, street corners, and card games—just to feel recognized and a part of something. But that doesn't change our deeper sense of wariness in the wider world.

When you understand a black man's history of lack of recognition, you are beginning to understand him. The recognition you are giving him may seem appropriate to you, but it may not be enough to overcome his history of slights.

Satisfaction: The Power of Feeling Rewarded for What You Do

James knew he was a damn good technician. But he rarely felt satisfied enough to say, "I like this job!" Every time something went wrong with the equipment people came running to him for answers. But no matter how often he demonstrated what his coworkers called "another one of James's miracles," he always felt used. He never was rewarded for his genius, nor did it really elevate his stature within the workplace. Everyone was friendly, but he always felt a little on the outside with both his white and black coworkers. He felt the white coworkers were threatened by his skills and the blacks were envious of his reputation as the technical wizard. There was no convincing James that things would not have been different if he were a white man with the same talents.

James wanted more than recognition as the "fix-it man." He gained little satisfaction from a reputation that led to no substantial rewards in the workplace. His fame was a hollow acknowledgment of his talents.

Black men like James are more likely to get the kind of consistent engagement that produces satisfaction by coming together in our sanctuaries, be they barbershops or churches, than by going to work. Places of brotherhood create more reliable circumstances for genuine recognition that is especially gratifying.

Legitimacy: The Power of Feeling That You Belong

If you're getting enough recognition and satisfaction, you tend to feel "this is where I should be."

Teddy, who had just transferred from a large midwestern state school to Hampton University, an historically black university, made that comment to me. It was not only the size of the state school that contributed to Teddy's decision to transfer out, but the fact that he did not experience acceptance among the student body.

Sonny, another young man for whom belonging was key to satisfaction, was one of the employees at a plant where people of color constituted only 10 percent of the workforce. Men of African descent were an even smaller minority. In his second year at the job, Sonny knew most of the employees of color as either friends or passing acquaintances. His skills were highly regarded and he was the beneficiary of workplace rewards, but he couldn't help feeling that this wasn't the right place for him. The talk around the plant was that workers of color had only recently been hired in any noticeable numbers. Moreover, he was privy to too many informal discussions among the African American men at the job about how uneasy they felt around the white workers. Sonny found himself second-guessing his decision to select this job over another where African American men were less isolated and where the atmosphere was more welcoming. He had chosen this job because it paid more money. Now he wondered if money should be the driving decision in selecting a place of employment.

Feeling that they belonged in the big picture was crucial to Teddy and Sonny. Any manager or diversity officer at a school or workplace would do well to understand this. Institutions that recruit African American men need to know that many of the activities and places we gravitate toward and remain loyal to can be understood in terms of how legitimate they make us feel.

This shouldn't surprise anyone, since there are many analogous situations. A primary recruitment strategy of inner city gangs is to make the youth feel a sense of belonging. A minister's congregation legitimizes him or her. Voters legitimize politicians. Wives legitimize husbands. Husbands legitimize wives. And for family members the family legitimizes. If you identify mainly as a "brother," (in the black male club) then like-minded men of African descent may legitimize you, but if you don't, or if other black men are not available to you, then you will need to be included by and embraced by significant others whose authority and influence you respect.

Validation: The Power of Feeling That Others Share Your Views and Values

Tim walked up to the bar where his friends had gathered for drinks and threw his coat on top of the counter.

"Hey, you guys. I just had several white folks pass by me, including a police car, casting suspicious looks in my direction. So what did black folks do evil in the news this evening?" His sarcasm continued with a smirk, "So, did we create a news event, or was I just getting the usual black man's treatment?"

It is important to know that others think like us. We come to count on our friends sharing our view of the world, providing us with "sanity checks," a frame of reference, and a necessary personal sounding board. When we stand on the corner to listen to other men's stories, trials, and tribulations—or nod approvingly to both the music and lyrics of our favorite rap, soul, jazz, or blues song—it confirms for us that we are not alone. We are not, as a member of my support group puts it, *"ter-*

minally unique" in the way we experience and view life. The beauty of feeling that you belong to a group is that you know you will share common experiences and outlooks.

Without others to verify reality, people become uncertain of themselves, even confused and disoriented about what is right or wrong. This is no less true for black men than for any other group of people.

Respect: The Power of Feeling That You Are Being Treated as a Person of Value and Worth

I met Tom at a diversity-training seminar that I was conducting for a major company. During the lunch break Tom came over to my table and asked if I had a few moments to talk. He knew I had to prepare for the afternoon session, but he rarely had the "chance" (read "safe place") to share some of his real work experiences with anyone other than his wife. I was a professional, an African American, a brother who seemed to know about the challenges of black men in the corporate world, and he knew that I could probably give him professional advice on how to handle a frequent occurrence. He thought he could count on me to understand who he was.

In his work group Tom repeatedly offered his opinion and views on solving conflicts, team building, and developing plans to increase efficiency and productivity. However, he always felt that his contributions were not taken seriously. One day his friend, a white coworker, rephrased the same suggestions Tom had made and pointed to Tom as the originator of the idea. But his white manager credited his white friend with the good idea. Tom felt humiliated and angry. He would be the first to say that being respected is a vital part of feeling like somebody. That's what Aretha Franklin's singing R-E-S-P-E-C-T was about to him as a man, despite what it meant to her as a woman.

The popularity of the saying "don't 'diss' me"—short for "don't show disrespect for me" among many African Americans—also speaks to the rules surrounding the violation of interpersonal boundaries and "my space." "Dissing" is linked with the behavior of urban youth and the street codes they follow, but as easy as it is to identify this value with the younger generation, it also represents the macho bravado attitude at all ages. Those of us who are older also expect and demand respect from those we encounter.

Our family, friends, and coworkers should know, moreover, that we want to be respected according to the standards we set, each of us, individually. Sometimes our "boys" (friends) define our standards for respect, and sometimes we set standards driven by our unique needs. A black male who needs reassurance that he is important, for example, may feel respected only if his plans for the evening are followed without question. Another's desire for loved ones to make a fuss over him and indulge him might come from his own sense of inadequacy, or a lack of enough indulgence or sufficient recognition from his friends.

If we are feeling disrespected when we leave one location, such as work, and enter another location, such as home, only to feel disrespected there, then the stage is set for getting upset and perhaps acting out. Respect is part of the nuclear core of our identity, and when that core is tampered with our entire set of protective instincts is activated.

"My clean boots are an extension of who I am," explained Jam, an articulate sixteen-year-old. "Anyone step on my boots, they're stepping on me, and I'm going to step on them." Assaulting someone for stepping on your shoes sounds crazy, even when the thinking behind it is understood. But when it comes to black men, respect is often the nuclear core of personality.

Rappers aren't the only black men who talk about the hazards of getting "stepped on," "trounced," "kicked to the curb," or "kicked in the ass." These are only a few everyday black idioms that represent disrespect and symbolize being down in the gutter in defeat. Being defeated, "whipped," means you can't hold your own under attack. You are vulnerable, and therefore weak. This is as much the case when you are verbally abused as when you are physically attacked. Survival and respect are heavily linked.

Respect implies mutual understanding and reciprocity among black men, based on an implicit consensus tied to our sense of right and wrong, as well as of social justice. But, for the individual, that standard frequently evolves from a lonely and complex experience of consensus building with other men of African descent trying to make sense out of life.

People who want to connect to us do well to realize that we are forever alert to the many ways we are disrespected, and we feel compelled to demonstrate our ability to fend them off. If we don't, we see ourselves as persons without dignity, people who have no pride. And that is an identity we cannot accept without losing self-esteem.

Dignity: The Power of Feeling That You Are a Person of Value and Worth

"Say it loud, I'm black and I'm proud," James Brown shouted out on behalf of generations of black men. He knew that a brother defines pride for himself. For black men, the most important ingredient in the definition of pride is the individual person's point of view.

Consider Wheels' story. He set up a makeshift curbside auto detail business in front of his apartment house on a Brooklyn street. It was one of his many hustles to make some extra change, to pay bills, and to indulge his taste in clothes and women. Everyone in the neighborhood knew that if you wanted your car to look nice you let Wheels work on it. Wheels also had to establish his own standards to preserve his dignity and reputation. You knew he would treat your car no differently than he would treat his own.

When Wheels purchased a new car, he expected all of the brothers in the 'hood to recognize his new car and heap praise on his selection. When he ordered many custom features he knew the car salesman couldn't appreciate what it meant to his reputation. With the special interior upholstery and stereo system, he had one of the "baddest" four wheelss in the neighborhood. When his car was finely detailed and polished to perfection by his secret technique, Wheels marveled at how everything else came together. He was gratified that everyone stared at the car's magnificence, and Wheels knew his reputation was going to remain intact and his opinion would still be valued. If you wanted to know about taking care of cars, Wheels was the man. But there was no questioning his work, for to do so would bring his honor into question.

You can't have dignity without self-respect. Likewise you can't gain dignity unless you have all the other elements working in concert to support pride in yourself. Wheels earned his dignity through his car. The personal achievement brought him the honor he associated with manhood. This is important to understand, because it helps explain the lengths to which someone like Wheels will go to preserve his dignity, even though everyone may not share his standards.

Pride is personal. Anyone working with or helping black men needs to understand that the idea of pride is not broad and inclusive. What defines pride for one person may be sorely inadequate for another, or out of reach for yet another. No one knows what makes a black man proud unless they ask.

Identity: The Power of Feeling Comfortable with the Way You Are and with Who You Are

Paradoxically, black men persist in trying to set standards for pride among themselves. Our relationship with women is a good example. "Where's your pride, brother?" was the challenge tossed at a member of my support group by the other men in the group when he admitted losing an argument with his wife. This was a challenge I have heard numerous times.

"Am I who *we* are?" That's a question some black men frequently find themselves asking defensively.

Dejo, for example, told me how he could lie wrapped in the darkness of his unlit bedroom, staring into the black hole of the night. Reflecting at first on his activities of the day—his accomplishments, uncompleted tasks—his thoughts drifted into evaluating his entire life. He thought about how little people really knew him. On the other hand, he also thought about how little he let people get to know him. It was not easy being a black man, he thought. A misstep and you could fall off the precipice into the abyss of presumptions about all black men.

I can understand Dejo's problem. Racial identity came hard for him, but it has rarely been easy for any black man. Think about the many ways we labeled ourselves over generations: colored, Negro, black, Afro-American, African American, people of color, biracial, people of African descent. These various labels reflect just how elusive our identity has always been. Some of us who are obviously of African descent quickly de-identify from America's racial history, saying, I'm Bajan, Jamaican, Trinidadian, Puerto Rican, or Dominican. All this shifting could lead anyone to ask, *Will the real "we" please stand up?*

Men like Dejo lie awake at night trying to figure it out. You know they have given up—and given in to invisibility—when they say, "Let's not talk about my identity as a black man, African American man, or man of African descent."

The problem with de-identifying is that it opens the door to greater ambivalence, a breeding ground for the invisibility syndrome. Without a positive sense of racial identity, it is hard to get a permanent foothold in the struggle for visibility.

In contrast to Dejo's view, most black men find that bonding with each other in various types of friendship networks strengthens self-esteem and confirms identity in the midst of invisibility. For the majority of us, a sense of brotherhood creates a safety net. It enables survival. It emphasizes looking out for one's self at the same time that it offers a significant number of opportunities for developing personal power within the ethnic group.

As an antidote to invisibility on the job or in our family relationships, brotherhood offers numerous protective environments and alternative places to be ourselves. That's a good thing, but it also takes its toll because empowered manhood is our ultimate goal. At its best, brotherhood is an avenue to manhood, not a substitute for it. When a "brother" knows he can achieve any goal he chooses, in any context he chooses, without giving into the worst effects of invisibility, he is on his way to real manhood. Manhood is implicit in the spiritual resolve to make commitments, and the sense of responsibility and accountability to keep them. When our feelings, thoughts, and behaviors serve the interests of our family, friends, and community—not only our self-interests—we have achieved what I mean by manhood. In other words, our manhood must be defined and evaluated by how well our relationships, family, friends, and community prosper as we prosper. To achieve this, our manhood identity must have at its core consensus, stability, and consistency in our commitment to beliefs, values, and behaviors, as well as our responsibility for their realization. Our manhood, therefore, must be greater in vision and practices than our brotherhood. Manhood thrives on personal power, it is not just a measure of it, but, like brotherhood, it turns on self-acceptance.

Self-acceptance came hard for Dejo. He wondered if it was right or wrong to identify with other black men. My answer was that it was not a matter of right or wrong but more a matter of how he wanted to conduct his life. The point was to understand his goals and then to be honest about the results.

He wanted to be somebody and to feel like a person of worth just like everyone else. If his efforts to achieve that fundamental identity were blocked down one path by invisibility, it was only natural to seek it down another through brotherhood. At the same time, Dejo was right to pause when he reflected on the mindless thinking and selfish "get over" behavior he associated with black brotherhood.

One time I asked Craig, a small-time neighborhood drug dealer, why he sold this stuff to the young people on the block.

"Look, brother, if I can't deal here I'll go deal in another neighborhood, but at greater risk," he replied. "If you don't understand what I have to do you won't understand why."

Both Craig and Dejo were trapped by the paradox of brotherhood, one abusing and the other doubting his identity as a black man. The idea that brotherhood itself could be problematic for black men struggling with invisibility reminded me of a lesson I learned as a child at the beach. Back in those days, I loved to build structures in the sand. Waves coming in and going out would flow around, through, and over my sculpted canals, mountains, castles, and barriers. I was fascinated to see how water from a wave followed my makeshift paths but also overran those furrows that were too shallow, creating uncharted outlets in the water's ebb and flow and destroying those I thought I had carefully created.

Like water running free, we either navigate the predetermined course or make our own way. Where we leave our mark, others will follow. If we make the mark too shallow, or make no mark at all, we will be swept away, leaving nothing in our place but dismembered dreams. Unfortunately, we often let ourselves get faked out by the paradox of brotherhood.

On one hand brotherhood is powerful, offering a substantive identity through which to shape our attitudes, opinions, and behavior on the road to empowered manhood. Brotherhood tells us how to relate to others, how to live our lives, and what to do differently than we might do otherwise because we are black and we are men.

On the other hand, brotherhood, in and of itself, won't necessarily block the invisibility syndrome or turn us into responsible men. Why? I believe it is because the messages, images, and patterns ingrained in our minds about the way to be authentic black men—what I call the brotherhood rules—are as likely to be infected by invisibility as stereotypes are. Opinions about how to be black men with respect among other black men—opinions that we are programmed to trust—may not be essential to our survival, but rather connected to some other agenda.

What is the self-identity of African American men who call each other "brother"? What social codes or rules merely mask a sense of invisibility and feed into the syndrome, and which actually contribute to our personal power? These are not easy questions to answer without intimate knowledge of the social world of black men.

2

THE BROTHERHOOD RULES

Learning How to Be

As a child growing up in Brooklyn, New York, I spent most Saturday afternoons with my friends, sitting in a movie theater. Whenever a black person appeared on the screen a tingling sensation rushed over me. I was exhilarated and eager to see what this person was going to do. Usually, the actor was a maid or a butler and largely ineffectual. Nevertheless, I left the movie feeling good. I had at least seen a black face on the all-important movie screen. I had made the best sense I could out of the images and messages that were available.

Already catalogued in the back of my mind was every useful lesson I had ever gleaned from my young life about black men and about how to be one—or not. I was insatiable about gathering these lessons. The alternative was looking stupid for not already knowing how I was supposed to be.

My friends and I were constantly customizing those lessons. When they didn't fit our circumstances, we preferred to go it alone rather than ask each other for advice. If all else failed, we resorted to improvisation. Already, the survival goal was clear: to preserve our dignity and maintain our respect—particularly our self-respect—and to gain recognition, satisfaction, validation, and a sense of identity.

Our ethnic identities were constantly being influenced by successive little satisfying experiences, some packaged and marketed in the form of media messages and images, and others passed on in places close to home. The rules gave us access to the black male's club, the brotherhood. Simple phrases and ideas, easy to understand and remember, but packed with subtle meaning, connected us to each other and the world of the men we admired.

The Black Male Vibe

To the casual observer, black male identity appears to be conditional in very superficial ways—ability in athletics, style of clothes, appearance, and language. These are ostensible attributes for bonding and acceptance. However, it is in the emotional intangibles of the "brotherhood" that we find the primary glue in the relationships of African American men. Friendships coalesce around shared (verbal and nonverbal) expressions of these intangible messages. They operate as a dynamic in a place full of men of African descent, as well as in the catching of the eye of the only other brother in a room filled with non-African Americans. This happens despite one's level of racial identity or income. It is the "black male vibe."

The fact that any aspect of it might be problematic, or may become our undoing as adults, never crossed my mind as a child. Nor did the possibility that there would ever be a generation of black men for whom it would become corrupted and passé. For me, brotherhood was like welcome rain, central to my self-identity and aspirations as I came of age. The brotherhood rules offer a priceless kind of closeness based on our belief in the sanctity of certain male privileges (such as authority, leadership, and knowledge) and the imperative to not waver when challenged, to be strong, to have heart, and to be brave in all undertakings. Ours is a macho bravado creed of self-reliance. It is drummed into us so effectively that we develop a self-righteous belief in its infallibility that can easily turn confidence into unreasonableness. The success of our journey toward manhood depends on sorting out the mixed messages. Here are some key examples.

"Keep Grounded": The Message of the Black Church

If you want a marvelous snapshot of healthy black male identity, I recommend you visit a thriving church in a black neighborhood. For me, the best theater of everyday black life always was and still is the black church. There, all the variety and vitality I found missing in movies, or for that matter in other media, flourishes on Sunday mornings and throughout the week.

My church was a place where African American talent and knowledge could shine and be displayed with support and fanfare. Every person's efforts and contributions were respected, his or her dignity preserved, identity nurtured, competence acknowledged, and visibility prized.

Reliable lessons in self-mastery and self-esteem were taught routinely. I witnessed men using their power as deacons and trustees, participating in all of the church activities, and exerting leadership in the social activities of the congregation.

For example, my father, the pastor, designed numerous ways to raise funds, particularly the cook-offs our various church clubs would sponsor. Every year, the North Carolina Club would try to "out-barbecue" the South Carolina Club. Similarly, other church clubs joined in friendly competitive social events for the purposes of fund-raising and spiritual fellowship. To prepare for those events, men and women would labor, digging barbecue pits, purchasing food, arranging the facilities and transportation, and making sure everything went off without a hitch.

The men in the church understood that they were in charge. They were keepers of its economic viability, leaders in every way, and they taught the children to be responsible by assigning little chores that kept us out of the way and yet fostered our sense of belonging.

For men who still follow this tradition, little has changed. As ministers and church members, black men and women work side by side for the common good. We are building large congregations, constructing new church buildings, creating community development corporations, and providing leadership in the community.

Churchmen tend to be powerful and influential in many other organizations in the African American community. We organize and provide the same type of leadership to clubs, fraternities, businesses, neighborhood and school committees, and local politics.

Talented African American youth assuming organizational leadership within high-risk youth gangs and managing a street drug trade are exhibiting comparable management skills. If the skills youth use to survive in the street were evaluated in legitimate businesses and turned to legitimate ends, they would be cited for managerial excellence. They, too, are grounded; but, unlike brothers in the church, they are not grounded in anything of value. Young leaders in family clubs, such as Jack and Jill of America, Inc., in fraternities, informal social clubs, church and school clubs, and gospel and hip-hop music business ventures come closer to the intended message of the rule.

While it is also true that African American men find many legitimate leadership opportunities in mainstream society, the basic danger is uncoupling our leadership from the social, familial, and spiritual vision the church represents. In the church, a brother who stays grounded watches out for the interests of the whole community, even when he pursues opportunities for his own gain.

"Know the Scoop": The Wisdom of Storytelling

My pastor likes to tell stories about his personal experiences and those of others he meets as he carries out his various duties. One Sunday he talked of being pulled over by the police and how quickly he let them know that they had stopped the wrong man.

"It would have been one of their (the police) worst days on the job if they had detained me much longer," he said. Given his working relationship with the chief of police, the governor, and other community officials, this statement was not overblown. The congregation laughed knowingly and approvingly of the boldness and confidence of our pastor's behavior. We had all been there in some fashion. His story showed strength of character, the confidence to defy intimidation, and the courage to stand up against erroneous assumptions by acting on what you believe is right.

Black life is replete with stories of confrontation with and resistance to authority, as we struggle to maintain our dignity. African American men have come to learn how to be themselves in and out of the African American community through hearing them. They teach lessons and give guidance about personal relationships, intimacy, power, revenge, protection, making money, and just plain everyday survival as a black man. Whether hearing them from the pulpit, at home, on the street corner, at parties, or through song, they become a beacon, showing how to handle confrontation, how to feel about it, and how to maintain self-respect.

We learn as children that to be a man we must be respectful of what legends tell us, legends formed from the trials and tribulations of survival by previous generations of black men. Some of those legends directly instruct us how to confront racial indignities. They include the powerful legacies of Denmark Vesey, Frederick Douglass, W. E. B. DuBois, Martin Luther King Jr., and Malcolm X. Favorite legends teach moral courage, such as that of Muhammed Ali, who refused to enter the armed forces because he was a conscientious objector. He was stripped of his heavyweight title, but he held firm to his position until he ultimately prevailed. We identify with winners when we learn about the *Amistad,* the Tuskegee airmen, or the highly successful Negro Baseball League, by just hanging out with our brothers on the street corner.

Many of the brotherhood rules for preserving respect and dignity come in stories, tales, and exploits of legendary folk heroes such as John Henry. But contemporary heroes are emerging. Consider the entrepreneurial accomplishments of Reginald Lewis who, through a very sophisticated buyout, acquired one of the largest companies in the world. The title of his popular autobiography is *Why Should White Guys Have All the Fun?*

Rap music continues this tradition. It is fresh but not new. Embedding messages into stories, rhymes (toasts), and song has been an African and African American tradition for centuries. Crafting conventional wisdom out of particular personal circumstances and placing that knowledge in stories and songs is commonplace among all people of the world.

For example, the stories of African American men being wronged by white men teach that attempting to get even is very risky business. Even though I often heard people counseling that, if you are wronged, "Don't get mad, get even," I learned from those same people to weigh the risks involved in protecting my dignity. Songs and folktales taught me how to respond when confronted by intimidation from peers, gangs, and other adversaries.

My youthful partners and I used to sing and chant in rhyme as we were hanging out on the stoops of Brooklyn. At that time, we did not know we were following the tradition of African people. One day, gang members of the Chaplains jumped Pee Wee, the smallest boy in our group, thinking he was a member of another gang, the Bishops. Later, as Pee Wee dramatically related his near-death experience and feeling of helplessness, our friend Randy said, "Man, you need to follow the wisdom of the signifying monkey." Pee Wee asked "What's that?" And Randy rolled out in syncopated rhythm one of many verses.

Down in the jungle near a dried-up creek
The signifying monkey hadn't slept for a week
Remembering the ass-kicking he had got in the past
He had to find somebody to kick the lion's ass.

The tale of the signifying monkey is that of an apparently powerless small creature getting over on the lion and other large jungle animals. The examples the monkey illustrates show us how to level the playing field when confronted with problems and danger. The selection Randy chose to quote spoke to Pee Wee's situation.

We all fell out laughing at the way Randy could put things into perspective by reciting this simple tale. To revenge humiliation or personal attack, "Go get your boys."

Black men in barbershops, pool rooms, gyms, pick-up games, parties, or standing on the corner continue to tell more stories and jokes to achieve status in the group than to convey life lessons, a problematic practice for the goals of manhood.

"He's Got Game": Playing at Teamwork

Hoop dreams are emboldened through endless tales of the court. They raise unrelenting hopes that our talents in basketball will become a way for us to acquire money and stature while doing what we like to do. For us, basketball is as much a conduit to a better way of life as it is a leisure activity; but it symbolizes more. It is an arena approved by most black men as a legitimate place to demonstrate our measure as men. Of course, herein also lies a very big problem—because not all African American boys are interested in proving themselves through basketball, even though we all know that the game has the brotherhood seal of approval. But the game is widely embraced, because we have easy access to it and can legitimize it with our own playground rules and schoolyard athleticism. We know how to do this. There is history to our expectations—legends that inspire possibilities, people to model our skills after, and repeated challenges to overcome. Playing basketball, if you are decent at it, can be a confidence builder. It provides us with dreams, and it dangles the lure of rewards that come from making genuine efforts—in spite of the small odds for making it to the top as a professional, much less a superstar athlete.

When opportunity eludes us, passes us by, or runs its course, we are prone to look to our dreams, or live in embellished tales of what coulda, shoulda, woulda been, "if I only had gotten this one break." Being caught up in what might have been frequently obscures the possible, which is why hoop tales seem endless in the brotherhood.

One holiday weekend several of my partners and I took our young sons, nephews, cousins, and their friends to a park to shoot some hoops and chill them out until the barbecue was prepared. We played some feeble games with them, trying not to embarrass ourselves by showing our age. While we were in the schoolyard court, some young men in their twenties arrived and challenged us "old-timers" to a game. Much to the chagrin of our children, we accepted their challenge. We ultimately beat the youngsters using the old team strategy of "give and go," humiliating them in front of their girlfriends on that warm and sunny holiday afternoon. It was sweet "in your face" revenge. Since that day we have relentlessly boasted about it to our wives and friends.

That day surfaces in our narrative whenever we get together. For each of us it has taken on legendary proportions. It is clear how that moment tapped into our pride and feelings of competency and power. Despite the fact that we had never played a game together before, we were not surprised that our friendship could help us exploit our long-standing bond and find a way to face down this potential defeat. By putting a game plan together that we each knew would work, we enabled ourselves to tap into our inner resources and pull out skills and stamina in more cooperative and unselfish ways than we often experience in the daily use of our talents.

One particular message in basketball is that teamwork gets results. This rule applies easily to our relationships with each other in sports. However, outside that arena, we are less sure of ourselves and less trusting of each other. We are not as familiar with winning strategies or as practiced in the skills required. We are not sure of the talents we need to use, or we choose not to use talents we possess. We falter if we don't have the proper personnel around us to bring out our best efforts. When we don't have the right people around us ("our boys"), or feel that we are in the right place ("our corner"), we become guarded and defensive.

Our talents and resourcefulness are greatly enhanced when we work together toward a common goal, but it only takes the occasional incident to puncture the bubble of security we have created in our individual worlds, to bring out our propensity to hide within the comfort of our personal worlds, to shut ourselves in, and to shut others out.

"Don't Get Blindsided": Accomplishments May Not Mean a Thing

When Carlos, a former corrections officer, remarked, "I just do my job. I can't get caught up in what other people think or say about us [black men]," his friend Dave replied, "You may feel that way, but what others think may make a lot happen around you." Dave was trying to get Carlos to see the unfairness in how black men are treated. He wasn't a "paranoid junky," as Carlos would frequently label him, he just knew what he knew, even if he couldn't always prove it. Even when we keep to ourselves, do our own thing, something can happen to pull us out of the comfort of minding our own business. Proving what we know or sense about inequities is a rite of passage for African American men.

In the fall of 1999, as reported by the New York *Amsterdam News,* a Harlem-based newspaper, the NAACP announced a class-action lawsuit against Cracker Barrel Old Country Store, a restaurant chain, for discriminating against African American employees. "Plaintiffs described widespread discrimination against African Americans in hiring, firing, pay promotions, and terms and conditions of employment."

If this were an isolated incident, there wouldn't be much concern; but, for the African American community, it is the repetitive occurrence of such incidents that provokes anxiety.

On June 7, 1998, in Jasper, Texas, James Byrd Jr., an African American man who was walking home, was accosted by three white men, tied in chains to the bumper of a pickup truck, and was decapitated while being dragged along three miles of a bumpy country road. The men were tried and convicted of their brutal murder—but as so many African Americans (and white Americans as well) saw it, it is as shocking and enraging as it is disheartening that such incidents can still occur. To us as black men, these incidents are often seen as a direct challenge to our ability to protect ourselves and our loved ones from those who vilify and hate us. We smile and silently cheer as a group of armed black men parade their indignation under the resurrected banner of the Black Panthers, even as we watched our current black leaders confront the authorities demanding justice. For some of us, the emotions stirred by these incidents fester; others dismiss the incident as an isolated occurrence and try to get on with life, while for others these concerns transform into vigilance, preparedness, and action. Whatever the reaction, the bottom line remains the same: here is another incident where we are being disrespected, or worse still, treated with gross inhumanity.

Learning that six African American Secret Service officers were involved in a racial incident, the group I was counseling was incredulous, almost unable to believe it. "Secret Service men?" they muttered.

The officers had stopped in a Denny's restaurant in Annapolis, Maryland, to order breakfast. The delay in service they were then subjected to was so blatant that the officers were compelled to file a discrimination suit. Subsequent disclosures uncovered a nationwide pattern of "blackout" at the Denny's chain. This management-sanctioned practice systematically denied service, required payment prior to orders being served, or prevented access by African Americans to Denny's restaurants. Numerous claims from all around the nation by other African American individuals and groups formed the basis of a class action lawsuit that United States Justice Department attorneys concluded was the largest case ever in the history of the public accommodations section of the 1964 Civil Rights Act.

Some of the amazement at this triggering incident was because of the power, influence, and stature we attribute to members of this elite law enforcement branch. We would like to believe that they have attained an unassailable status. We learned differently. There is no such job status—not one that offers absolute immunity from hurtful attitudes. "How could they be treated this way? How could they be so helpless?" were the troubling questions presented by the men in the group. "Hey, they're black men," one brother blurted out quickly. He also looked at us with an attitude of slight disbelief that we were even asking those questions with the obvious answers.

As the men recalling this story observed, it is hard to miss a table of six black men seated together, particularly when they loom so conspicuously in a sea of white customers. Thus, the intent of the snubbing was to deliberately ignore them long enough to make them disappear—to force them to walk out in indignation, perhaps proclaiming to never again visit Denny's. But the very act of snubbing is indeed an acknowledgment of their presence, and therein lies yet another peculiarly African American male paradox. It is disturbing to be present but not seen, and it is disturbing when our presence is seen as disturbing.

This cabal of humiliation offered millions of black men a lasting lesson in "Racism 101." The image of these black men waiting and waiting and being deliberately and obviously ignored delivers an enduring message, not only about the way we can be treated but also about our worth as human beings and as citizens of this country.

"Accomplishments don't mean a thing" is also part of the message here. Such open and premeditated acts of racism further imply that education and intellect, even when put to good use, have no currency when possessed by African American men. Moreover, it raises the shadow of "intellectual inferiority" for anyone who remembers the incident, long after the event occurs.

Just as I can speculate on what the Secret Service men went through as they were waiting for the service that never came, I can also imagine what happened when they left that restaurant and continued their day and their lives. Each man, separately, had to find a personal way to regain his dignity and self-respect. He had to examine how he personally responded to the circumstances and somehow find inner peace with his actions. Each man had to consider what message this incident and the behavior of the men in his group conveyed to those who witnessed it, and to those who subsequently would learn about it.

In incidents of this nature, African American men must cope with a primary psychological challenge: finding acceptable ways of contending with anger, then indignation. A subsequent need to act on it can be a very private hell, if we persist at going it alone.

"Don't Act Your Color"

As you have seen, responding to invisibility involves three things: adjusting our criteria for being seen or not seen, scrutinizing others' criteria for inclusiveness, and discerning the difference between tolerance and acceptance. Invisibility suggests that if there is a script that white people must follow, there is a script that black people must follow. In this drama, rejection is only a subtext. Something else is always going on. In the age-old conflict between mothers and sons about how to behave in public lies a classic example of how unintended messages about invisibility, privilege, and acceptability become encoded. Nathan

McCall, in his autobiography, *Makes Me Wanna Holler,* relates one such lesson learned on a trip with his mother to a restaurant.

> Even some of the grownups who set out to arm their young with racial pride seemed haunted by contradictions, which their children absorbed. Whenever we were going to restaurants or other public places where a lot of white folks would be around, my mother insisted that we get meticulously groomed and pressed beforehand, and when we got there she reminded us (it was more of a threat) to sit stiff as soldiers and be quiet. Every now and then, if one of us dared to cut up in public, Mamma would yank him firmly by one arm, pull him to within an inch of her face, and whisper through clenched teeth, "Stop showing your color. Stop acting like a nigger!"
>
> My brothers and I would sit solemnly and watch as rowdy white kids entered those same public places, shirtless, barefoot, and grimy. Their parents gave them the run of the joint, allowing them to stomp, shout, scream, do virtually anything they wanted, including tear up the place. I envied their freedom and craved the specialness that excluded them from our self-defeating burden: It seemed we were niggers by birthright and destined to spend our entire lives striving in vain to shed that rap. But white people could never be niggers, even when they acted like niggers with a capital "N."

Nathan McCall's mother was concerned with how her children's behavior reinforced stereotypical assumptions when that very same behavior in young white children was, in fact, a statement of privilege. Imagine what difference it might have made to Nathan's young and developing self-concept if his mother had admonished him with, "Stop acting like those white children. You are of African aristocracy; we behave differently." A message built on positive images within our own majestic history conveys another kind of message, and is more likely to fortify inner self-esteem. If our own standards of self-acceptance have consensus, we will be less concerned about meeting those set by others.

"If You're White, You're All Right": Self-Defeating Messages of Inclusion

African American males know they are up against the prevailing white American image and "criteria" for being an acceptable American. This is yet another variation on DuBois's concept of "double consciousness." But the paradox in this message is that we can become more tolerable— visible—if we meet the criteria of being less black, that is, more white. African Americans maintain a strong faith that education is the bridge over the barriers that skin color constructs. On the other hand, we know that education is not an unconditional pass to privilege. We want to be-lieve that education will neutralize skin color and bestow legitimacy. But we have been disillusioned by too many examples to the contrary.

Tim, a twenty-year-old, was referred to me by his parents. They hoped an African American psychologist could help him. Tim had lived in an integrated suburban community since age ten, and now his parents were concerned about his life direction. Tim was floundering in college. His parents were embarrassed that he showed no interest in the African American community or its history, in spite of their encour-agement. Moreover, Tim was not clear about his future, wanted to drop out of college, and struggled with friendships and his racial identity. He had encountered problems of acceptance with the white families of the girls he wanted to date in his predominantly white high school. Now at a prestigious college, Tim found himself caught between white student friends and the black students with whom he was identified, more by association than by genuine friendship. His father's solution was to send him to his old alma mater, Howard University, an environ-ment he felt would remedy both his racial identity problems and his ed-ucational aimlessness. This was a defeat of Tim's family's plans, since his father had worked and sacrificed for years to enable Tim to get an Ivy League education. Tim would be forgoing an opportunity his fa-ther had worked hard to provide to his son.

Tim did not appreciate his father's solution, since he felt that "black colleges are not necessary, because we can go to any school now. Any-way, I find my white friends accept me more than the black students, who always like to stick together and are not friendly." Tim's father, who cringed at this comment, remains bewildered as to why Tim feels this way. "He thinks nothing like us," his father often reflects. "It was a bad decision to move the family out of the city to the suburbs. But I was only thinking of Tim's welfare and future opportunities, to help him to make it as a black man in this country. My wife insisted on seeing a counselor, but I still feel we can work it out ourselves."

Tim's father was haunted by his decision, as he watched his son take what he considered an uncharted and undesirable life course. He realized that many of his personal decisions had been made in reaction to what he thought was conventional wisdom, or, as he put it in a painful admission, "what helped me to get by in white society." But in seeing his son develop an identity that did not value his African American heritage, Tim's father questioned his own motives for moving to the suburbs, as well as his child-rearing style. He viewed his wife as an accomplice in this matter, as she had downplayed the importance of linkage to the African American community once they left the city for the suburbs. Tim's father had even begun to question his choice of a spouse. It became apparent to Tim's father that he was as much running away from stereotypes associated with blacks in the city as he was pursuing opportunities he associated with living in a integrated suburb.

"Don't Mess with Me": Projecting the Defying Spirit

The picture of black male students at Cornell University in 1969 armed with rifles and bandoliers of ammunition and standing in front of a building was published in every newspaper and magazine around the world. That image is a classic of the twentieth century. The students were protesting the unequal treatment experienced by African Americans. This act represented a dramatic escalation of our swelling national discontent. The picture conveyed a poignant message of defiance. It captured a particular aura of black masculine defiance. Pictures of Bobby Seale and Huey Newton together personifying the arrogance of the Black Panthers projected the same spirit.

I was supervising a local youth program one day when Steven, a fifteen-year-old, walked into the community room to sign up for a trip the group was taking. He wore the teenage urban uniform—baggy pants and jacket, heavy boots, red bandana, with a reversed baseball cap on his head.

"Sorry, Doc, got caught up in scaring a few people on the way over here," he said after I commented on his tardiness. I asked him what he had done.

"Nuttin, just walking."

This interpretation of black male behavior is typical. For example, Jerome, at twenty-two, was trying to get on the police force and had been referred to me by the local branch of the Black Guardians, an organization of African American police officers. Jerome came to me because his personality tests and interview for the police department had raised concerns about his suitability for law enforcement. He was told his profile suggested that he had some underlying and perhaps unresolved anger that might prohibit his effectiveness in performing his duties as a police officer. Jerome noted that they were concerned about his suspension from high school for fighting, and other difficulties with school authorities.

Jerome's outspoken nature had been carefully documented as discontent by school authorities. Jerome says he was merely fulfilling his role as a student leader who was expressing student concern over the school's unfair treatment of black students. He admitted that there were some provocative incidents "that got a little out of hand." The school principal viewed Jerome's acts as those of a troublemaker. After an eloquent attempt to justify his case, Jerome just threw up his hands: "Look, Doc, what black man doesn't carry some anger?" Jerome understood that what he thought was the right thing to do in the past was now compromising his career opportunity.

We know that our body language can project attitudes that can be disconcerting to others. But a defying spirit is at the core of our masculine image. Look closely at rap videos and you will see the same defying spirit that was projected by the Cornell students. We put it in our rhythmic movements, we make pointing gestures to accent the attitude; the "look" and husky vocal tones underscore the importance of our message about our inner strength. It is an unmistakable declaration. Inevitably, the defying spirit is a part of how we approach and how we must interact with the world. *Expressing* it can be the dilemma, because it can also be a trigger excuse for our repression, or a barrier to opportunities.

"I'm Bad": Swagger as Confidence or Arrogance?

Recently I was walking behind three teenage black males and noticed how their swagger was basically composed of the same movements I perfected when I was a teen. And it struck me how this walk has persisted over time, how young black men and even adult black men have maintained it as a natural part of their gait. Of course, each generation wants to claim they invented being cool. I found myself falling back into that old swagger, rolling my shoulders in synch with a dip and bounce to my steps. I wanted those young men to look back and see their stride had nothing on mine. I often fall in that very same walking style as I navigate some of the neighborhoods of New York City where I work. The swagger is an expression of many things. It represents confidence in yourself, belief that you can take on anything, and a notification to others that "what you see is what you get," a sheer rhythmic energy exuding might.

We all smiled when Richard Pryor and Gene Wilder, in the movie *Stir Crazy,* were being placed in a jail cell. Pryor, encouraging Wilder to mimic him, swaggered into the cell saying, "Yeah, I'm bad, I'm bad," as he confronted new cellmates. Black comedians have frequently incorporated "black male swagger" into their routines to convey "the attitude." But it is more than a comedic routine. It is one of our kinesthetic mechanisms for reinforcing self-confidence, signifying an arrogant readiness for any challenge.

"Keep in Your Place": Playing the "Race Game" at Work

In 1994, a group of African American employees with Metro-North Railroad claimed the company was guilty of discrimination, after an inordinate number of workers of African descent were unceremoniously fired following years of service. The employees' attorneys claimed that "the railroad's chief career-wrecking technique, it seems, is a time-honored and highly effective one: digging up some tiny transgression—and then bearing down on the black employee like a roaring locomotive." It has long been understood by African Americans that employers will build a case to fire black workers by focusing upon what, for whites, is often a minor employee infraction. This history perpetuates the messages of power and authority, saying to African American employees, "You have no control over your fate; therefore, stay in your place."

In a similar fashion, African American officers with the Immigration and Naturalization Service were kept in check. Kellogg Whittick, the first black officer to advance into the senior ranks of the agency, noted that following his retirement in 1983 no African Americans had moved into upper management. As reported in a 1994 *New York Times* lead article entitled "Black Officers in I.N.S. Push Racial Boundaries: Borders and Barriers," John J. Washington, a senior special agent, commented that "the problem is that the good old boys still treat this agency like their clubhouse. And they still don't want to let us into their club." The article further reports that "as black immigration officers tell it, they are consistently denied promotions for which they are qualified. Excluded socially from a tightly knit corps, they end up being ignored for the special training and assignments that enhance careers. They are disciplined, suspended, and dismissed more than their white colleagues. And when they filed Equal Employment Opportunity complaints, they said they suffered retaliation." Mostly, the black officers see a subtle racism, "a racism of exclusion," in Mr. Whittick's words.

For these men to be summarily dismissed reflects the truth about the nature of their acceptance in their workplace. It is difficult to be fired. But to have your dismissal follow years of productive service and to know that it was engineered by deceit and unethical behavior is disillusioning. You call into question your ability to survive the racial terrain. We must successfully navigate that racial terrain, not only to remain competent providers for our families, but to maintain our self-esteem as men, publicly and within ourselves.

Many African American men today tell me that surviving in their jobs involves constantly contending with the symbolism of their presence. We must moderate any assertiveness so that we are not labeled aggressive. We must not be too dependent upon supervisors, so that the presumptions about hopelessly incompetent black men are not reinforced. We must be twice as prepared, and we must demonstrate appropriate language skills, so that assumptions about our intellectual inferiority will not easily prevail. When we join in joking and levity we must guard against having our wittiness perceived as our "real" talent. And when we are friendly to white women, we must be mindful of what white men think of black male sexual prowess, and also how feelings of betrayal can be triggered in the hearts of black women.

Not knowing how to act in the face of these attitudes in the workplace, and many other public settings for that matter, can be very confusing, stressful, and infuriating. Many black men have long given up on the notion of any genuine acceptance outside of the brotherhood, and only look for tolerance to get through the day. Many black men avoid playing this race game at all. Some of us look for places where other black men have found success in making money, gaining public recognition, and the apparent power to influence either the larger society or the African American community. Seeking success in the media or sports presents a very public and seductive opportunity. So, too, does the drug business.

"If I'm Seen, I'm Somebody": Hiding the True Self

Entertaining others has always been a socially tolerated form of visibility for African American men. This is as true within the African American community as it is outside of the community. However, the classic theatrical legacy of black men in entertainment as comedians is too often a caricature of black men. It serves to deepen the mystery over who we genuinely are for those who have no authentic, intimate contact with us. We also can become so enamored of the payoffs that come with wearing comedic masks that we start to behave as if they had real and positive meaning for us.

All too prevalent in television, the comedic roles of black men, in ways big or small, continue the stereotype of the blackface minstrel. Court jesters have never threatened the power of the king. Our antics are amusing distractions, unrelated to matters of state, matters central to meaningful inclusion. We know that on one level, but we like the money and attention it brings, nevertheless.

Likewise, African American actors in supportive dramatic roles rarely get to explore the reality of the black male experience. There is a black face, but not an African American man. The real black man is obscured, as our "normalized" media character compensates for (but is often in total denial of) any unsettling feelings that may be derived from our skin color. It is too uncomfortable to explore how whites, or others in these dramatic moments, would really respond to looking into the eyes of a black man—and, more importantly, how the black man would truly respond to that gaze, given the way we are often treated, and given our tendency to hide who we really are.

Let's not minimize what the portrayal of black men in movies conveys to those who watch. Many young African American men view media as a viable means through which to showcase their talents and have some aspects of their life experiences represented. It is a legitimate path out of private discontent. But it endangers other minds.

"The Gold Ring Is Everything": The Perversion of Values

Like media, the sports arena also neatly mixes images and messages for the African American male in a way that confuses our understanding of genuine recognition and acceptance. The glamorous lifestyle of a professional athlete is so attractive that we don't mind jumping through hoops to reach this goal. We dismiss and defy the reality that becoming a professional athlete (a picture that hangs on the wall of our minds), like becoming any other performer, is a very narrow passageway to visibility. Indeed, performing in the sports arena is not an opportunity we have created for ourselves. Nor is it connected to altruism or any underlying value or strategy that will rescue the community from the trappings of its invisibility, or the selfish motives that form our pursuit of opportunities in sports. On the contrary, it is a circumstance that is created in support of the national community's leisure, personal comfort, and business profits. The number of African American men who do succeed in professional sports and acquire material wealth is infinitesimal, when compared to the overwhelming majority of black men who barely make a fraction of a percent of what these athletes earn.

But aspirations to the "gold ring" of the champion create perverted values in the minds and hearts of young black boys. Their thinking is crafted by the glitter of the improbable, and this, too, becomes a definition of recognition—recognition built on dreams that are not likely to be fulfilled. Success on the field or court has not translated into equivalent success in coaching or front-office jobs where the heart of the business is located. Black youth are unable to see how much the professional entertainer or athlete is like the gladiator or the court jester of old, with no publicly valued persona outside that arena—who are useful only as long as their productivity on stage or on the athletic field endures.

Was this not the premise for pacifying slaves? Allow outlets of hope to keep them happy; provide scraps from the table so they feel better-fed; permit marriage and family to elevate intimacy; offer work in the big house as a privilege. But, despite these little gratuities, the slave was still a slave, because it all could be taken away at the whim of the master.

It is a cruel hoax to hold up the achievements of role models, when the chances of achieving a similar success are so slim. Furthermore, keeping hope alive with improbable goals distracts us from focusing upon the ones more likely to be achieved. Linking recognition and acceptance to lofty, jackpot goals with incredible odds blinds African American young men in particular to the value of aspiring toward more achievable, sustainable ones. Why? Because, in a big way, we want to get out from under poor circumstances and have a better life. We become so frustrated with our efforts toward the impossible dream—the longshot—that despair and hopelessness are the results. We question our judgment and ability to realize our dreams. Trust in the American dream is badly shaken. It is not into the eyes of the role models who are comedic, sports, music or business superstars we ultimately must look, but into our own. That recognition is the first step to restructuring our self-image so that we might attain realistic goals. But it also means recognizing how the role models we have chosen to identify with achieved theirs.

Acquisition of material possessions by the African American middle class is rarely attributed to sacrifice, hard work, commitment, and responsibility. Having resources that characterize being middle class is not represented often as one of the sources of leverage in leadership, or as being vital to political influence, community development, or control of personal destiny. Rather, the black middle class seems to be held hostage to caricatures and innuendoes that suggest phoniness and betrayal, in spite of its material resources and expanded life options. Some black middle class males feel that is an unfair burden, others don't care; but a significant number are very conscious of lending their shoulders for others to stand on, regardless of opinions about their middle class image. Being a part of the black middle class, therefore, also means struggling with invisibility and a credibility gap.

"Don't Get Too Big": Failing to Thrive, Despite Being Middle Class

One of the great dilemmas of brotherhood is the love-hate relationship we have with education, money, and career success. We have trouble accepting the lifestyle that middle-class status can create, so we embrace it cautiously at best, because of the conflicted feelings and challenges it stirs up. We fear rejection by those among us who have significantly less. While there are striking images of what material wealth can provide, we all share the experience of persons with financial resources leaving the community. Even though a common public aspiration in the African American community is to get out of our poorer neighborhoods, one of the concerns is that the transition also includes the risk of losing a connection to our roots, our intrinsic feeling for our people, our legacy, our history, our struggles.

In other words, the goal to be visibly successful often comes with rules of acceptance that can distance us from those who have not achieved in a similar way. The quest to be legitimate can lead some of us to deny our origins. As their income grows, the gap widens between those men who have chosen education and career and those who are the middle- and working-class poor. The distrust, anger, and suspicion just below the surface can emerge and divide us. This happens in spite of the fact that history repeatedly demonstrates that African American men in the middle class—educated, with financial and political resources—have provided leadership to nearly every historic movement for our civil, economic, and human rights. Nevertheless, black men today can feel profoundly guilty about achieving middle-class status, or troubled about how to relate to other African Americans without the same resources.

Will owns a barbershop and beauty salon. His business was very successful, so he moved to New Jersey and purchased a five-hundred-thousand-dollar home in an integrated suburban community. But he felt so guilty about his purchase that he deceived his customers by allowing them to believe that he still lived in the neighborhood. He even fabricated a story to his extended family, his aunts, uncles, and cousins, about how modest his new community was, so that they would not envy him or think he had gotten "too big" for them.

Carson, at forty-five, is very self-conscious about how he displays his material possessions. He drives around in an old car, dresses modestly, and gives no indication of his wealth. His wife, on the other hand, makes him cringe at how she flaunts the expensive gifts he purchases for her. This difference in style, which he admits comes from his self-consciousness over whether he deserves this financial success (given "all the other brothers out there struggling"), has been a source of conflict in their marriage.

A pretentiousness label, or the implication that "You have become too big to associate with me" ("me" being the poor and working class of the African American community), is a liability that has become associated with middle-class status. It is part of the great psychological divide within the African American community, where worthy contributions are hidden behind assumptions and misunderstandings related to privilege. Feelings of envy, denial, and abandonment can entrap us all.

E. Franklin Frazier, in his classic *Black Bourgeoisie,* portrays moneyed African Americans enthralled with conspicuous consumption and mimicking white society. These images support certain attitudes today. It should also be noted, however, that some aspects of these attitudes harken all the way back to the days of the house slave and the field slave. Lawrence Otis Graham, in his book *Our Kind of People,* takes a journalistic look at the African American upper-middle class and argues that there is no monolithic black middle class, but, instead, individuals and families diverse in resources, influence, and interests. They live at a level their income provides. They indulge; they harvest the rewards of generations of educated, prudent business and professional decisions, and they are families very mindful of and active in their contributions to and leadership of the African American community. But until the worth and contribution of the African American middle class becomes widely accepted, the transition to this status will continue to be achieved with ambivalence.

Eric slipped into the McDonald's bathroom in his regular afternoon routine of changing from his prep school clothes into his homeboy clothes before getting close to his neighborhood. It's a similar exercise in the morning going to school. His sister Carolyn does something similar on the way home from parochial school. In explaining his behavior, Eric was clear that he did not want to seem too privileged to his friends and neighbors.

Lorraine Hansberry's play *A Raisin in the Sun* still best captures the complexity of family feelings and ambivalence about moving to a better neighborhood, particularly when it is integrated and such a move suggests abandoning our roots. After Walter Lee, her son, loses the money for their house and their dreams, Mama thinks aloud as she laments that the family will not move.

"Lord, ever since I was a little girl, I always remembers people saying, 'Lena—Lena Eggleston, you aims too high all the time. You needs

to slow down and see life a little more like it is. Just slow down some.'
That's what they always used to say down home—Lord, that Lena
Eggleston is a high-minded thing. She'll get her due one day!"

In *Our Kind of People,* Lawrence Otis Graham shared some of the
same apprehensions a number of the 350 people he interviewed for his
book had about telling their stories. It is revealing about this dilemma of
having wealth, being privileged, middle class, and of African descent.

A great proportion of the individuals that I interviewed—
whether they were former debutantes, leading physicians, or
powerful Fortune 500 executives—initially expressed a desire to
remain anonymous. While, ultimately, most of them agreed to
speak to me on the record, many of them insisted that whites and
blacks of a different class would attack them for acknowledging
the accomplishments of their families or of themselves. Many
had been raised to apologize for their success and for their am-
bition, even though equally accomplished relatives had preceded
them by several generations. While they willingly spoke about
success among their black colleagues who participated in their
ninety-year-old fraternities, cotillions, social clubs, or summer
resort activities, they remarked that such discussion was unwel-
come among outsiders.

Apologizing for who we are or what we have become is deadly for
working together. Until we gain comfort with our identity—particularly our competencies, strengths, and achievements—we will continue
to lessen our effectiveness as a community against common injustices.

The Problem of Brotherhood

Certainly when we look at our circumstances today we can say that we
have come a long way. Why be so hard on us, Doc, you might ask?
Viewed within a historical framework, our emancipation from slavery
has not been that long ago. Our shaping a relevant African American

brotherhood is a process still in its early stages. It has, after all, been less than a hundred and fifty years since Abraham Lincoln freed our ancestors, after their enslavement for over three hundred years, beginning in the so-called New World with the trading of captive Africans to the colonists in 1517. By contrast, cultures in Africa and on other continents have had thousand of years to develop their societies and distinctive roles for men and women. It is no wonder we are still at it.

No matter how we rationalize our current state of brotherhood, it contains too much self-destructive behavior and favors wearing far too many masks for our common good. When black men act like strangers to each other, we seem unfocused and undisciplined as a group.

"Be number one." "What have you done for me lately?" "What's in it for me?" These messages imply that we are running competitively alongside the rest of our materialistic, achievement-oriented society. But we lag far behind whites as a group by every objective measure of personal wealth. To what extent is racism the culprit, and to what extent are we? Not facing this question only perpetuates our invisibility.

I believe that brotherhood, at its best, is a viable gateway to authentic visibility and empowerment. African American men have too many life experiences and strengths in common to ever need to make the journey to manhood in isolation from each other. More of us must find a way of coming together for our mutual benefit.

Why is it so difficult? What keeps some men from moving beyond the "What's up?" and stopping, embracing, saying to each other, "Let's get it on"? Based on my analysis and experience, what stands in the way is our profound if understandable refusal to give up any further measure of trust, power, or control than we must to maintain our cool masks, or macho bravado, in the face of invisibility.

3

DILEMMAS OF TRUST, POWER, AND CONTROL

Seduced into Believing

There I stood in the middle of the street with a gun stuck into my belly by an intimidating fifteen-year-old who was looking me dead in the eye. He wanted to know what I was going to do if he decided not to return my tape recorder, which was clutched tightly in his hand. I was a graduate research assistant working on my master's degree, and at that moment I could only think that I had chosen the wrong profession. "Lord, if I can talk myself out of this predicament, I will change," flashed through my mind. My idealism, fueled by the passion of the civil rights movement, had me on these streets seeking to better understand black adolescents who lived in the ghetto. My research was centered on the question of what distinguished the lifestyle of delinquent youth from nondelinquent youth.

For the past year I had lived in this Washington, D.C., high-crime neighborhood, conducting my research by meeting and interviewing the young people in the surrounding area. The gun-toting kid knew me and I knew him. We had played ball together. Sometimes he won, sometimes I won. Today he was challenging me, and I knew it. We talked, parried with words, engaged in the ritualistic dance of street survivors. Finally, he gave me back my tape recorder.

But this encounter had not been about the recorder, it was about trust. It was also about maintaining his authority, or power, by holding on to his privileged status. He had been my neighborhood assistant, and now the project was over and the equipment had to be returned. I was about to change his life in an instant with my request that he return the tape recorder. An assistant one day, just another street kid the next. He knew the year was a momentary experience in both of our lives, but I am certain he hoped that our relationship would have a different outcome than all the relationships in his past that had fallen apart. He felt that I had made a promise to him; now I had pulled the rug out from under his feet.

For me, that dramatic moment was a perfect snapshot of our experience of trust, power, and control as men of African descent. I think that, like my street assistant, we sometimes hold a gun to the belly of racism, angry over betrayals. Our private lives are no different. We make commitments and build up expectations, only to discover that our privileges can vanish just as quickly as they appeared. We are shaken by disappointing outcomes and ask ourselves whether venturing outside our comfort zone was worth the risk of our self-respect and dignity.

Repeated disappointments lead us to doubt our capacity to control our destinies, or to bring about any positive changes to improve the quality of our lives. Doubt undermines our judgment and compromises our ability to judge the genuineness of our experiences with others. We become so preoccupied with our past failures and those of others that we cannot focus on what might actually bring us some relief. My assistant, for example, felt I valued him above the other hoodlums on the block; the opportunity that I had provided had made him feel special, and he expected a certain amount of permanence to follow from his gains. By taking the recorder back, I inadvertently implied that he was not respected and valued. He felt that he had been used and he felt foolish for having expected anything other than that I would take advantage of him.

Too frequently black men end up feeling like suckers for having thought we were valued, only to find out that we were being exploited. As soon as our usefulness ended, we were discarded. Eventually, we become leery of anything that looks like an opportunity, mistrusting its genuineness and permanence.

Learning to Expect to Be Betrayed by Society

Most people expect that if they act a certain way, this or that will follow. Black men cannot rely on this principle. Even when we act a certain way, we are often not treated as expected. As brothers often tell me, if you get a good education, it does not mean that you will get a good job. If you are a good worker, it does not mean that you will get a promotion. If you are a good family man, it does not mean that you will be supported as a father or husband. Try to be a good friend, and you risk betrayal.

The way we conduct our daily lives twists into a knot of possibilities and disappointments. Things never quite turn out the way we expect, so we begin to expect that they won't turn out, even though we don't stop hoping. Between rounds of possibilities and disappointments, we hold onto our code: Don't get taken, tricked, or duped. If we reveal doubts about ourselves, then we come under suspicion from other brothers. Thus, we are likely to become jaded and angry.

Black servicemen can tell you about returning home from the world wars, Korea, Vietnam, Desert Storm, and everyday duty, only to encounter discrimination and mistreatment at home, in spite of our growth in numbers and authority in the military.

It took the United States fifty years to recognize the heroics of Lt. John Fox, who, in December 1944, sacrificed his life by ordering his own men to fire on his position to stem an enemy attack during a battle in Sommocolonia, Italy. His aged comrades of the black 92nd Infantry Division were happy he received the Medal of Honor in 1997, but they still feel bitter about the insufficient recognition of the outstanding combat records of many more black servicemen. Black servicemen from the Revolutionary War to the present have had to reconcile the mission of serving their country—and possibly making the supreme sacrifice of giving their lives—with the reality of how they are treated

ꙮuntry they are defending. Examples of extreme racist re-
returning black veterans of World Wars I and II are numer-
his book, *Journey to Liberation,* historian Dr. Molefi Asante
꙯s this about returning World War II veterans:

"Arriving home from the battlefront, African Americans were often
in more danger in their own country than they had been in Europe or
Asia. On July 24, 1946, four African Americans—two soldiers who
were only recently honorably discharged from the United States Army
and their wives—were lynched in Walton County, Georgia. Two
weeks later, another brutal lynching of an honorably discharged
African American soldier occurred in Minden, Louisiana. It was revealed later that the former soldier refused to give a white man a war
souvenir that he had brought back from overseas. For this refusal he
lost his life to a mob of whites."

Of course, most reaction to the returning black veteran throughout
all wars was not so blatantly horrendous. But returning veterans have
consistently faced the same patterns of discrimination and prejudice
that permeate the overall society. Countless stories of our allegiance to
persons, ideology, or organizations, sometimes at great personal sacrifice, end in dishonor or betrayal, breeding disillusionment at the least.

Michael Eric Dyson, noted scholar, professor and author, writes
about a profound childhood experience that shaped his view of himself
and other black men throughout the world. In his book, *Reflecting
Black,* he tells of the impact Martin Luther King Jr.'s death had upon
him.

"I will never forget the effect of King's death on me as a nine-year-
old boy in Detroit. For weeks I could not be alone at night before an
open door or window without fearing that someone would kill me, too.
I thought that if they killed this man who taught justice, peace, forgive-
ness, and love, then they would kill all black men. For me, Martin's
death meant that no black man in America was safe, that no black man
could afford the gift of vision, that no black man could possess an intelligent fire that would sear the fierce edges of ignorance and wither to
ashes the propositions of hate without being extinguished. Ultimately

Martin's death meant that all black men, in some way, are perennially exposed to the threat of annihilation."

This event nurtured in Dyson problematic lessons about trust, power, and control. For many who put hope in the civil rights movement, Dr. King's assassination created more profound mistrust in this nation's capacity to change.

Who Can We Trust?

One evening I was reading a children's book to my seven-year-old son. It was about Dr. King and Malcolm X. My intention was to be "the good black father" by reading to him and teaching him about black history and culture. When I was done I searched for another book to continue my reading. My son looked up at me thoughtfully.

"Dad, they spoke out to help black people and they were *killed*?" Focused on sorting through his cluttered pile of books, I said, "Yes that's right." Suddenly I realized what he really had said. I knew I had to say something more. I needed to help him better understand those tragic circumstances for these great men, while not overly frightening him. I struggled to collect my thoughts on the matter.

"*You* speak out for black people. Are they going to kill *you*?" he blurted out. I was shocked.

Tonight he had learned something that was not the object of my lesson. Nevertheless, it proved to be a powerful lesson for both of us. I wondered what other conclusions and concerns the passages I had just read brought to his keen young mind. How did it influence his view of the world? How did his voiced concern for my safety as his father affect his concern for his own safety? My next thought was chilling. I wondered if my precious young son thought me incapable of protecting him, if I could not protect myself.

My son's question raised the issue of trust. Could he trust my ability to provide a safe environment, to be able to protect him and his mother, his brother, and his sisters? Could I guarantee these things if I took such public positions on civil rights as did Dr. King? He relied upon my ability to provide stability in his environment, a prerequisite to helping him develop confidence in the next morning being not much different than the previous sunrise. His was the world of a trusting child. If caring for him required me to be less public, not try to fit in, to become invisible, should I comply, so as to reduce his childhood anxieties? And I was concerned because I knew that these were challenges that he, too, must face, more directly, as he matures.

Trust means acquiring confidence in people, institutions, and systems, as well as stability in our expectations of our world, and from people to whom we are attached. Out of experiences with trust we evolve expectations, exemplified by the importance of a best friend keeping his word when he says, "I've got your back." To trust is to depend on expectations. When there is doubt, or considerable cynicism, we question our personal power. Seeking self-respect, we confine trust in our capacities to those things we *can* make happen in our life.

If I did not want to limit my son's capacity to trust, I needed to make him feel both safe and capable of pursuing his dreams and ideals.

Where Can We Assert Our Power and Control?

Author Sylvester Monroe writes compellingly about power and control in black men's lives. Recalling a reunion of his childhood friends, Half Moon, Honk, Pee Wee, Steve, and Billy, Monroe reports on the survivors of the Robert Taylor Homes in South Side Chicago, a tough inner-city housing project. In the book *Brothers,* Monroe and Peter Goldman, journalists for *Newsweek* magazine, tell the up-to-now life stories of the friends. They list their accomplishments and tell of their personal trials and tribulations—twenty years of challenges in a neighborhood fraught with risks to survival. Some, like Monroe, achieved success in the professions or in business. Others escaped the projects with more modest success, with homes, good jobs, and families. Others, like Steve, remained in the old neighborhood, secure in the world "where you know your way around."

Power for black men is linked to the ability to come through new experiences with few spirit-breaking moments and with our dignity intact. It is hard to force us to take on new experiences if we feel our spirit might be broken and our dignity damaged. When we do take on new relationships, activities, and opportunities, it means we are certain about handling the risks to our sense of personal power.

In my experience, black men will play any game as long as there is a fair chance of learning the rules. When the criteria for recognition and rewards are clear, and the invitation for inclusion seems genuine, brothers can have real confidence that success is possible. Understanding the real rules, the real agreements, is essential to our sense of power as black men, whether in the streets, the corridors of an executive suite, or in relationships with black women. There is security and comfort in knowing "the name of the game," the do's and don'ts, the ins and outs—particularly if it brings success and peace of mind with few hassles. If you control the rules you control the game. Our relationships as husbands, fathers, and friends are entangled with that preconception.

We define success as the ability to demonstrate control over our reality. Bill, the corporate manager, continuously displayed his dominance over his family to affirm his authority. Other men define their masculine identity this way; but, as brothers, the terrain of control matters more. We need relationships and activities where we feel valued as men *and* as persons of African descent. For that reason, we seek arenas where we can bring competitiveness to our play—such as in basketball— assertiveness to our work—such as when we try to outsell our coworker—bravado to our love life as "Mr. Big Stuff" or "the Player," or natural confidence in being the best storyteller/rapper, performing only under those circumstances where we can rely on knowing the rules and predictable outcomes.

This need to "know the deal" is reasonable. If we learn as boys and men that the environment outside of the brotherhood and black community is not to be trusted, we are less likely to invest ourselves there.

Guidelines for Parents, Teachers, and Mentors

Never doubt the power of positive, realistic, black male role models who can demystify the wider world beyond the brotherhood and show healthy trust, power, and control in action.

My father and uncles told tales of overcoming racism to teach us children about how dreams are won in the face of adversity and betrayal. In particular, Grandpa's life story told us that determination can control destiny, that belief in your own vision, judgment, and ability—in spite of what other people say—leads to power. We were taught to trust ourselves—even while others try to steer us in improper directions and toward unworthy goals, because of their ignorant notions about what young black men can or cannot do. And, through these examples, I was taught that fortified by a spiritual and religious faith all things are possible.

My patient Jerome illustrates the benefits derived from learning early on about trusting his own judgment. A tinkerer since his childhood, Jerome loved the inner workings of any machine. Electronic circuitry, or anything that made machinery work, fascinated him. On the other hand, his performance in school was a disaster. His scores on standardized tests in science and mathematics were average and his verbal test scores were consistently below grade level. Jerome was neither challenged nor motivated by his teachers. He became bored with school, did no more than average class work, and nearly didn't graduate. His school performance landed him in special education classes.

"I was labeled and tracked for nowhere, along with so many other black boys," Jerome said to me during one of our meetings. He was "tracked" for invisibility, with his talents lost in a school system that did not appreciate him for who he was.

When the computer age was young, in the early 1970s, Jerome, then twenty-one, became captivated with programming and the mechanics of computer processing. He became a self-taught expert in both computer programming and computer hardware. Undaunted by those who discouraged him, warning him about the complexity of computer language (which was presumably too technical for black folks like him),

Jerome found a coworker and future business partner who shared his passion. They worked together tutoring each other in this new industry. Eventually, through perseverance, some of the software they developed became popular. Jerome's white business partner was only interested in his talent, not his color. They eventually developed a very profitable business.

"But it was not easy," Jerome says. "I don't kid myself, or other young black men I try to mentor. I want them to know that getting to where I am today was no breeze, even with my talent. And I am gifted in computer science, as my software patents and income show. Many people tried to discourage me with stupid comments that computers were not for black people. Can you believe I heard that from both white *and* black folks?"

As Jerome's resolve shows, black men do have the power to control their lives. Other examples abound, whether it's the Tuskegee airmen defying beliefs about aviators of African descent, or black athletes breaking records believed to be unbreakable. And individual records of black male achievement don't stop there. Consider Dr. Benjamin Carson, one of the first neurosurgeons to successfully separate Siamese twins, or Dr. Neil de Grasse Tyson, the astrophysicist who heads the world renowned Hayden Planetarium, or Patrick Clark, who became a famous international chef—or any student who defies a teacher's low expectations and excels. Their success is a testament to their ability to trust their own judgment.

The Habits of Successful Black Men

Such men branched beyond arenas they knew they could control. They exercised power over their circumstances. They influenced or persuaded others to follow their particular way of thinking. They created plans of action. They made responsible decisions for themselves and others. They used their available resources, even as they confronted looming disappointments.

The eminent scholar and educator Edmund Gordon promotes the term "defiers" to describe their ability to:

* Exceed expectations
* Beat the odds against success
* Have self-confidence and believe in themselves
* Remain resilient and bounce back from difficult challenges
* Formulate a purpose and goals
* See the future in what they do today
* Be tough
* Be independent thinkers, but be able to work with others
* Learn from their mistakes
* Resist discouragement by those who disbelieve in them
* Make something out of nothing
* Convert challenges into opportunities
* Find ways to succeed
* Maintain a positive attitude
* Not accept failure
* Learn from others
* Be adaptable, flexible, and be able to make adjustments

When Jerome had experiences that made him feel invisible, he convinced himself that he had talents and mobilized others to help him to acquire the proper knowledge and skills that allowed him to become an information technologist. Others credit him as "beating the odds," but Jerome actually beat invisibility. It requires being focused on goals, committed to your dreams, and ingenious in overcoming roadblocks.

Defiers have an indomitable spirit and willpower to succeed. Jerome felt discouraged by people and circumstances on a number of occasions, but he persisted. The more barriers he met the more determined and resourceful he became. Jerome transferred to another training program when he felt he was not getting the proper preparation or treatment. It extended his months in training by half a year, and added more debt in the form of student loans, but he achieved his goal. He figured the added cost for proper preparation would be made up in the long run by better paying jobs.

The four main characteristics you see in Jerome and other defiers can be summed up as:

1. assertiveness
2. decision-making powers
3. determination
4. perseverance

Defiers do not capitulate. We refer to them as "beating the odds," but there is nothing magical or lucky about a defier beating invisibility. They come to terms with invisibility in ways that enable them to overcome mistrust, the fear of asserting power, and the fear of losing control.

The Defiers' Messages about Manhood

My grandfather owned a farm in Mississippi. In order to keep his property and make the loan payments, he had to guarantee that his crops would produce the maximum yield for sale. During my grandfather's time at the turn of the twentieth century, it was common for African American farmers to put up their entire farm as collateral for the much-needed seeds and supplies each planting season demanded. A misstep in farming could result in the loss of your entire farm in just one bad crop year.

On March 4, 1925, in Mississippi, my aunt and uncle borrowed $398. They signed the following deed of trust for the money:

> It is our intention by the above description of real and personal property to convey by this deed of trust all the land, lands, mules, mares, horses, wagons, plows, etc. we or either of us own and in Madison County, Mississippi. Whether properly described or omitted from this description all are covered.

Unfavorable agreements such as this one were common, putting blacks in the position of quickly losing their farms if the slightest thing went wrong. Such agreements were virtually unheard of for whites. My grandfather had twelve children, and they all worked that farm day and night—even the most reluctant of all, the ninth child, my father.

My father, like his brothers and sisters, was pushed by my grandfather to get an education and make something of himself—so he, too, worked hard day and night, attending Virginia Union University, Union Theological Seminary in New York, and Teachers College, Columbia University. He took a small church of a hundred congregants in Brooklyn and built it into a congregation of well over four thousand.

My brother and I grew up around his friends: Dr. Gardner Taylor, Reverend Sandy Ray, Reverend Adam Clayton Powell Jr., Dr. Samuel DeWitt Proctor, Reverend Vernon Johns, Reverend Martin Luther King Sr., to name a few. As adults, my brother and I realized we were blessed and fortunate to have known so many legendary African American men—often as routine guests around our dinner table.

We each watched our father and his friends making tough decisions during the civil rights movement. And we heard repeatedly the message that, in spite of the struggle, we could not let it deter our pursuit of dreams.

My father and his friends exemplified that message. They were intelligent, articulate, defiant—curve setters, every one.

Throughout my childhood I witnessed my father's countless meetings with individuals, groups, and organizations building bridges of understanding, taking on leadership roles, and launching new initiatives to better the African American community. He reflected Grandpa's value that you must be out—literally and figuratively—in the fields, and work day and night to accomplish something. Like my aunt and uncle's loan agreement, his message to me was that the "contract on life" for African American people may present obstacles to achievement, but *our* family legacy says that it can be done. *No excuses!*

Just like my father and his friends, there have been generations of defiers who have fulfilled all and more of the traditional expectations of manhood. Unfortunately, their stories too often go untold and uncelebrated.

PART TWO

ENTERING THE DANGER ZONES

For a Black man in this country, it is not so much a matter of acquiring manhood as it is a struggle to feel it is his own.

—William Grier and Price Cobbs, *Black Rage*

4
MASCULINITY AND SEXUALITY: THE MYTHS AND THE MESSAGES

The Box of Presumptions

I was startled. Unexpectedly, a man knocking on my office door filled the frame and blocked the light from the hall. In a few seconds I recognized Jim, the father of Darryl, the thirteen-year-old boy I was counseling because he was clowning around too much in class, being disruptive, and not performing up to his potential.

"Doc, I hope you don't mind this interruption, but I was in the neighborhood and thought I'd check on my son's progress." Jim's deep, rich baritone reminded me of the actor James Earl Jones. Moving briskly across the room, Jim towered over me. He thrust his hand forward, enveloping and covering mine like a warm mitt. I sat rooted in my chair, still a bit stunned by his unexpected presence. Jim released my hand and quickly sat down in a nearby chair.

At six foot eight, and weighing in at over two hundred and fifty pounds, Jim had his pro-football dreams dashed when he tore cartilage and ligaments in his knee during his second year in college. He never graduated, but often relived his semipro days, when he played and traveled with teams in the United States and Canada. Those stories frequently include Jim's continuing amazement at the response of others to his size, dark skin color, and deep voice.

His size and looks significantly determined his outlook on life, his career options, and being a father to his son. Wary of the true reasons for his inclusion wherever he went, his size made him feel self-conscious and overly cautious in making everyday decisions, personal traits he disliked in himself.

There had been a time when he thought his body size and appearance would bring him career and sexual opportunities. But he learned the hard way about being led, rather than being in charge of his own life. He battled being made invisible by what others presumed about him, offered to him, and took away from him when they were finished with him. He knew how it felt to be left with only disillusionment and disgust at being played for a fool. Jim felt a strong obligation to protect his son from the school of hard knocks and wanted to make certain that Darryl followed a clearer path to manhood.

Smiling knowingly—apparently trying to ease the surprise of his sudden appearance—Jim crossed his legs, greeted his shocked son, who was sitting across from me, and proceeded to describe how he happened to be in the neighborhood. Dropping in to see me was a not-so-veiled message that he was in charge of his son and family. In our fifteen-minute discussion, he wanted to get a quick summary of how his son was doing, and to let me know how much he loved Darryl and wanted him to stay on the right path. He wanted his son to see him as a father who was doing the right thing and being a good role model. It was important that I understood this. He did not want to be associated with stereotypes. He would not be overlooked or misrepresented. Being misrepresented was a constant theme in Jim's life. He battled others' beliefs that all he had to offer was what his massive size evoked in people's minds. He wanted respect as a unique person who was in my office to help me teach his son a lesson about being a responsible black man and father. He had a job as a stock clerk by night and worked days delivering Coca-Cola, and one day he hoped to purchase his own trucks and distribution routes. He was thirty-three years old, and he and his wife, Ann, also had a ten-year-old daughter. His shaky marriage had endured several separations.

The Myth of the Designated Talent—Jim's Problem

I've known many men like Jim whose skin color, size, and aura of masculinity create constant turmoil in their lives. Other people insist on what they are like and what they can do, despite being corrected when wrong. People act on and in these men's lives with little consultation, believing they are acting in their best interest—or, as is more likely, their own.

Since childhood Jim heard comments on his physical size. People, including family members, would tease him about how he was going to make *big* money as a pro football player one day. He resisted, with great personal stress, his uncles' pressure to enroll him in little league football as a child. His childhood interests were actually more invested in helping to repair the small appliances and household gadgets for his mother than in athletics. The pressure from his uncles about football, and his competing interests in mechanical things, foretold a lifelong conflict that Jim would repeatedly face—how to remain true to your interests when they go against others' expectations for you.

Jim's story is especially loaded for black men, given the prevalence of distortions and negative assumptions about our abilities. It suggests that teachers, coaches, partners, and parents who genuinely care about our welfare should be careful that their desires for our betterment do not overlook who we are—our true and different abilities, as well as our interests.

As children, it is difficult for us to go against the wishes of our parents, relatives, teachers, and coaches, once they have made their minds up. Like Jim, we can say, "I didn't know any better. I was a kid. When people took me under their wing they were very insistent." Sometimes it is easier to give in than to fight, particularly if you think people have your best interests at heart. This complicity creates a convenient and seductive partnership between your needs and their wants.

This seduction pulls us further into invisibility. Always seen as a "good, obedient child" by his mother, Jim found his tendency to please others a liability. Like Jim, a person with many promising talents can have all but one overpowered by what other people want. For example, people who thought Jim's size made him the perfect football player overlooked his mechanical talents. For Jim, the label of football player created conditional acceptance and brought him conditional privileges through association and inclusion.

Conditional inclusion, whether genuine or disingenuous, has attraction for many of us who want to be accepted as part of a larger social arena that offers attractive perks and privileges. Our human desire to be recognized and accepted on many different levels makes the rewards from succeeding at whatever society holds out to us seductive. Doing what society asks of us gives validation in ways that we are unable to gain in other areas, perhaps even beyond what our friends have achieved. This is because we are capable in the arena in which we are accepted, even though we have other talents.

Jim was both a genuinely talented athlete and someone with a mechanical aptitude that earned him the nickname of "fix-it man" among family members. But he could not find the same encouragement from others to develop his mechanical talent as he could to be motivated to steer toward athletics. Stereotypical beliefs about what black men can and cannot do corral us into preordained opportunities. In our decision making, we find ourselves leaning toward them for support, recognition, rewards, and validation. Any other talents or personal qualities that we possess are pushed aside for the sake of predictable glory. We can become swept up, overwhelmed, and confused. After a process of critical appraisal, we can realize that "this isn't me." Suddenly discovering the hypocrisy of our experience, we become disillusioned.

How, then, do we learn appropriate responses to this hidden danger? For example, Jim conveyed to his son in his brief but richly filled reflections that tall, well-built men are associated in positive ways with virility, strength, courage, competence, sensuality, and sexuality. He wanted his son to understand that these associations can also explode in his face. Jim does not want Darryl to be seduced into believing that the positive assumptions behind these associations always lead to positive outcomes for black men.

Darryl has the physical attributes that are so shrewdly exploited by advertisers of after-shave lotions, colognes, underwear, and more. The same attributes got Jim's coach and mentor's attention. But none of the people who loved his gifts had helped to prepare him to handle the other opportunities he had, or those that possibly lay ahead. He was coached in athletics, but not in life. No one had helped Jim understand how or why to be vigilant. By the time he figured it out in the school of hard knocks, it was too late for him to realize his life's dreams.

This was an important lesson Jim wanted to teach his son. The appropriate response to the hidden danger of being seduced today is to remain focused on tomorrow and have clear goals. Be vigilant and wise about the future, knowing that what you do today has payoffs for tomorrow. Assets and privileges at one time or place can be a liability later. It's not just what you do one time, but over time that counts.

Like so many others in his position, he had propped himself up with pride built on success very much shaped by society's expectations of him as a black man. But he also motivated himself with fears of being another black male stereotype, attempting to transform a negative belief that he was only good for athletics into a positive outcome. He was an exceptional athlete, good enough for elite professional sports, until his dream was shattered by an injured knee. But, alas, a time of reckoning had come: Jim finally had to face the fact that he did not know how to get himself out of this dead end, the one he saw his son now drifting toward—that would perhaps leave him in the future feeling as powerless as Jim feels in the present.

It was in individual sessions and a subsequent support group where Jim revealed the depths of his concerns. To his surprise, talking out his fears about his son and those heretofore undisclosed moments of personal powerlessness was both relieving and helpful. Those fears had immobilized him. If he wanted his son to be more resourceful than he, Jim had to figure out another way to create opportunities for himself and his son. He could not allow invisibility to cloud his vision of himself and limit his expression of his talents or his commitments to family and community.

The Myth of Criminality—Guy's Problem

Any accusation that "a black man did it" triggers deep-seated apprehensions that people will rush to judgment against us without adequate information.

From childhood, we are presumed to be impulsive, hyperactive, and unworthy of trust. By the time we reach our teens we are believed to be threatening and unpredictable. These beliefs are reinforced by a "criminality stigma" that further influences public assumptions about our aggression and need to dominate. The public whispers, "Can black men be trusted? Do we need to watch out for their anger and rage? Can we allow them to run things?" These questions are often answered with a rush to judgment that leaves African American men cautious and guarded.

Guy, a six-foot eighteen-year-old college freshman, knows that, wherever he is, if an APB (all points bulletin) goes out for a "large black man," he runs the risk of being stopped. Dripping with bitterness, Guy once commented on a police action reported in the newspaper in which numerous black men were stopped. "The public is reassured that crime is checked, seeing me spread-eagled, even though I'm innocent. But my guts are tearing up inside. I'm pissed off, frustrated, and upset by the humiliation. People do not understand what it does to me. I see no justification for stopping me, but my word is not good enough. It makes being a good man difficult."

Many of us see the rush to judgment of the public and the outcome from it as means of controlling black men. Consequently, we have to be vigilant about the power of snap judgments more than any other concerns in interpersonal encounters. This helps to create in us a leeriness about how genuine people really are, and it develops watchfulness in us about hidden intent. History justifies our vigilance and belief that we are especially vulnerable to false accusations. Consider the following examples:

Knoxville East Tennessee News (December 2, 1920)
SHE DENIES RAPIST WAS BLACK

MOULTRIE, GA, Nov. 30—Miss Bessie Revere, daughter of one of the most prominent women at Quitman, Ga., gained consciousness just in time to prevent the departure of a search party that had been formed to scour the country for "the big, black brute" who had been described in the press as her rapist. Miss Revere said the man who assaulted her was James Harvey, a prominent white man.

In 1992, Charles Stuart told authorities in Boston that a black man murdered his pregnant wife and shot him in an attempted robbery. Following a massive citywide search that focused primarily on the black sections of town, the arrest and detaining of hundreds of black men, and finally the charging of one with the murder of Stuart's wife, it was disclosed that Stuart himself was the murderer.

In November 1994, a distraught Susan Smith stood before a swarm of reporters in Union, South Carolina, and claimed a black man had carjacked her automobile and kidnapped her children. For days, black men suffered under the stigma of being suspects, until Smith finally confessed that she had locked her children in the car and had driven it into a nearby lake.

Such incidents create anxiety for the public and for men of African descent, exploiting fantasies and fears about our masculinity. As men, we feel we should not be afraid in the face of what has become an everyday threat—when we are in threatening situations, we feel that we should be able to get out of them intact. We should anticipate circumstances like this that challenge and threaten our manhood, we tell ourselves; a real brother would know better than to be caught off guard.

Experiences like this add up. How we manage our anxiety either reinforces or threatens our manhood. The process by which we manage anxiety becomes one of the agents solidifying our masculine identity. When we fear for our safety, the natural response is to protect ourselves. But when we do so in ways that are inconsistent with our image of being real men—such as swallowing our pride in humiliating and unjust encounters with authorities—it immobilizes our decision making and challenges our conception of who we are and what the brotherhood expects us to be.

Common sense says, when you're crossing a minefield, you have to watch where you step. When our identity is in danger, our tendency is to fall back on our code—that is, to try to think, talk, or fight our way out—or to draw upon the resources of brothers to assist us in getting out of trouble. We mobilize to deal with the tension and anxiety presented by the situation. This is a natural response. The challenge is to stay focused on our own positive value and worth without letting the experience we are going through corrupt us or break our spirit.

The Myth of Styling—Casey's Problem

One myth that explodes repeatedly in a black man's face is how much he lets his clothes define his sense of accomplishment. One client recently explained to me he could remember people admiring the massive strength and command he gave off just standing around in his football uniform after a game, particularly when his team won.

"We could get off on that jock thing," he said. "And we dressed with attitude when we left the locker room or hung out afterwards, a real fashion show. We were some bad MFs, and in charge."

Clothes can elevate our status by improving our rap, projecting a particular image, and implying competence. For generations men in the African American community have developed unique ways of dressing and acting to express masculinity and sexuality. Clothes are declarative; they help to state who we are, and to an extent what we believe. From zoot suits to leather suits to traditional African garments, our dress is important in making a cultural and gender statement. Our clothes are partly how we attract women and distinguish ourselves from other men. Our jewelry, hairstyle, shirt, pants, and shoes all fit within a brotherhood code for acceptance and approval. It is part of a carefully crafted style to win recognition for being a black man of distinction, and for having a particular identity that we create and feel positive in embracing. In other words, we are declaring our visibility on our own terms, a rule of brotherhood.

What the invisibility virus has done is to twist the means—styling—into an end, a false criterion for manhood. We favor styling as a criterion of our originality and talents, because finding satisfaction in it is more achievable than in other arenas, like playing basketball. Having good clothes is an achievable goal, perfectly attainable, even with limited resources. Approached with that attitude and purpose, our clothes easily become the object of a creatively distinct fashion, commanding admiration, imitation, and respect in our brotherhood. We cannot bank as much of our masculine identity on other more elusive goals, such as being a good protector, provider, or parent. Those goals which depend in part on our achieving success in partnership with others, institutions, and circumstances are less under our control. This is why some of us shy away from those less certain goals and challenges, given the jeopardy in which their pursuit places our masculine identity.

Casey, for example, had a hard time listening to the Manpower Training coach instruct him on how to dress when going for a job interview. He questioned the necessity of a shirt and tie, since it was not "him," and he questioned the identity of the brother who was trying to sell him on this requirement. Moreover, he did not like the suggestion that his Jordans were not appropriate shoes to wear. He fought the staff about the right clothes to wear for his interview, saying he only felt comfortable in his street attire.

The coach tried to get Casey to understand his reasoning by drawing the parallel to how gangs have their unique clothes that serve as a uniform. Many jobs require a certain attire that serves as a uniform. This was why he should follow their instructions about how to dress for his employment interview. But Casey was not buying it, because it was not who he was. Slowly, it became clear to the coach how much Casey's Jordans made him feel like a man.

Casey was no fool. He knew that dressing and acting the way others wanted for a job in a workplace that likely would not accept him was not being real. Why would he dress up to be something that he was not? He was comfortable with the way he was and felt no reason to compromise.

The Nike company banked on Casey's desire to be like Mike, the unbelievable basketball player, not like Mike the prudent businessman.

Mike's abilities to float and dunk were highlights of promotional marketing, not his self-discipline or business acumen. In other words, they did not show how Mike, to become powerful and rich, took control of his talents through unrelenting practice linked to performance, and made the sacrifices to be able to stay at the top of his game. Those values were not the goals of advertisement; they focused on values that would sell shoes, such as the need to identify with the established greatness of Michael Jordan, not the process that led to greatness. Exploit the hunger for gratification *now,* never mind about the future.

For access to a sense of brotherhood, bank on clothes. They are accessible and a commodity that instantly commands a certain kind of visibility. However, elevating clothes to define one's manhood is symptomatic of the struggle with invisibility. To be recognized as a dapper or stylish dresser makes many of us feel like somebody. Manhood, in contrast to modeling dress styles, bestows recognition from modeling commitment, fulfilling responsibilities consistently, or delivering on promises to elevate one's family and community.

Mistaking the Forest for the Trees—The Myth of Black Standards

Some of us are so busy keeping up with the popular expectations of black male behavior that we may fail to see better standards to emulate that are right in front of us.

For example, Trent grew up in a house watching his stepfather Jerome do everything for his mother. Jerome's love for her was unquestionable. He would help with household chores, frequently cooking for her when she returned from work late in the evening. When she was unable to get transport he would go pick her up. When illness flared up he was an attentive nurse at home and a companion who visited her hospital bed daily, bringing small gifts to cheer her up. His mother did the same for Jerome.

Theirs was a model of a loving partnership, something that Trent found frustrating to get others to believe was more than an exception. "You dote on him terribly," her sisters would frequently say. Trent knew otherwise, for many of his mother's and stepfather's friends had similar loving and working relationships.

It is easy for some of us to justify our way of being a man when appropriate models are discounted as exceptions, or when standards are defined only by current trends. Since trends are temporary and very much influenced by each generation, it is easy for us individually to exploit "wiggle room" in our standards and vacillate between what's in style today and the lore of black manhood that is passed down to us. Each generation contributes to trends and, thus, to their own history. If history, traditions, knowledge, wisdom, and manhood skills are not valued and passed on, we are susceptible to reinventing the wheel and not understanding why there is no progress.

Adewale (aka Steve) sat in front of me in a tailored black suit, a black no-collar shirt, a gold chain, and a red, black, and green bracelet, along with a Kente-weave kufi on his head. He was concerned about Simba, his son, who was hanging out with local gang members in the neighborhood. Simba wore gang colors and attire, as well as an attitude toward his parents for bringing him to see me. Adewale talked about what amounted to Simba's betrayal of his effort to raise him with African values, such as those represented by Kwanzaa. Simba talked about how none of his boys or their parents believed in "that African stuff," since "you get respect by taking no shit from anybody," not by rituals. He drew no connection between the rituals of his street life and what his father was teaching him.

Both Adewale, as father, and Simba, as son, were defending their standards of manhood. The father's were rooted in his own evolved African worldview and traditional parental authority, and Simba's was based in the realities of survival in a gang-controlled neighborhood. Conditions for recognition, validation, and respect were different for each and greatly determined by their generation. Each saw the other's chosen standards for being visible as a man as unsuitable, although each intuitively understood that the other's model represented his way of surviving with dignity as a man of African descent.

Lover and Dog—The Myths of Black Sexuality

In the movie *Shaft* the lyrics of the title song portray the detective as tough and sexual. "No one understands him but his woman," croons Isaac Hayes. Shaft is a "bad mutha—" and the character keeps true to this portrayal in every scene. All the brothers and sisters know what that means. We love it because of how it frames and presents a defiant, confident, and passionate brother. These qualities also make him appealing as a man and as a lover. He doesn't come across as a person easily tied to commitments, other than those that are convenient. In fact, we could easily see Shaft as a womanizer, "a dog," spreading his passions around from woman to woman.

What often stands for African American male sexuality are "stud" images. This is reinforced by figures about teenage pregnancy and fatherless black children in the black community. This is not a good image of our sexuality, and it powerfully overshadows any other realities of us as intimate partners.

The allure of the cool, sensuous male who has it all together, like Shaft, is very appealing in the brotherhood. This is a prized, special male talent—part of the aura of our black masculine mystique that some of us aspire to. This cool stud caricature, however, burns itself into the public's lens, supporting stereotypes about our abilities. To the public, we are what we pretend, or appear, to be. Being associated only with this image is not the way we want to be seen, and it is an image to be avoided, but feeling invisible, we seem unable to set values and rituals for our masculinity and sexuality that go far beyond presumptions and stereotypes. By contrast, defiers have a core of sacred codes, beliefs, values, and practices regarding manhood, that future generations of men of African descent would do well to follow.

I was doing some research about the resilience of African American male elders in Mississippi that took me into their homes. While I was setting up for one such interview, a wife noted how pleased and excited her husband was to participate in my study. "Nobody has ever asked him to tell his life story before," she said to convey how much my visit meant. His story covered thirty years doing maintenance work in a Mississippi sheriff's office. I sensed that there was a lot of sensitive history to his career. In our brief conversation, his wife let me know how he helped support their children, who all went on to become professionals. One son is now a presiding judge in the same district of the sheriff's office where his father suffered years of indignities. Generations of black men were detained and mistreated in that jail. She told me his story as she served me refreshments, telling me how her husband was defiant, confident, and determined in his family goals—while still remaining a loving man. She wanted me to know how appealing her husband was to her, with his dedication and sacrifice to family.

One story about black masculinity and sexuality is all too visible (Shaft, the heralded movie character), the other is not (the unassuming Mississippi jail maintenance worker and father of a judge). One story gets greater recognition and endorsement from the public by its resonating media appeal, the other, the story of a common elder, remains unsung—and when it *is* told it receives a cool reception. Many black males would fail to recognize and accept the virtues of manhood demonstrated by this maintenance worker in a Mississippi jail.

Which story holds the more viable criteria of masculinity and sexuality for men of African descent? Which story models courage and love better? In the struggle for control over standards for recognition and validation, which story better supports stereotyped notions about black men? These are tough questions, for in their discussion there is controversy about our criteria for authentic manhood. In controversy there is confusion, and it is in confusion that invisibility thrives, manipulating what we hold up as important in being a man of African descent. Why is it so difficult to concede that enduring sacrifices for a larger goal can be as appealing as a sensual swagger?

5

THE MISEDUCATION OF AFRICAN AMERICAN BOYS

The First Seeds of Frustration and Uncertainty

Sam leaned forward during one of our counseling sessions and recounted the following story with obvious passion.

He was seven years old, tussling with a group of boys on the neighborhood playground. A normal squabble over who should get a ball had developed, predictably for little boys, into a shoving match. Sam pushed a white playmate, who fell to the ground. The playmate's mother rushed to his aid.

"Leave him alone!" she yelled angrily at Sam. As she ushered her son away from the scene, Sam overheard her parting words to her sobbing son. "Be careful playing with black boys. They're so aggressive, and sometimes they hurt people."

Sam could not understand why she would say such a thing. He did not see himself as someone who would "hurt people." His young eyes filled with tears. Suddenly his mother was by his side. He told her what his playmate's mother said and asked, *why?* His mother responded angrily, telling Sam not to pay it any mind. She grabbed his hand and they left the playground hurriedly.

This childhood playground experience was Sam's first conscious signal that something might be wrong with being male and of African descent. This experience was painful and confusing.

Sam was the youngest of four children raised by his mother in a New York City housing project. A very hardworking and religious woman, she tried to instill in her children the importance of good behavior, hard work, and decency.

Sam was sensitive to his mother's anger and mistakenly thought it was directed at him. He overheard her heated phone conversation that evening with his grandmother as they discussed the incident. His mother's fury made it clear to him that the shoving match was no small matter. Years later, he still associated his playful tussle with this particular playmate with upsetting both his mother and grandmother. He had internalized the idea that he and his behavior were somehow bad.

Through adult counseling with me, Sam came to understand that he had been a victim, stereotyped by his playmate's mother. In the mounting drama, his mother and grandmother became unwitting accomplices by trying to inoculate him against society's unfair presumptions. The aftermath to the incident frightened and confused Sam as much as the triggering events.

Fears about Our Safety

The invisibility syndrome does not develop overnight. It starts with racial moments in which childhood innocence becomes secondary to safety. African American males learn at an early age that to be male and black is a matter of grave concern. We sense it by the way our families whisper about our behavior from the time we start walking.

"Don't you boys get into any trouble," our parents always seem to say. Although we do not want to think so, there is always something foreboding in that admonition—something that hints at a special concern. The implication is clear. Our safety is connected to how and when we make ourselves visible, particularly outside of the community. It is such a powerful concern that when African American boys want to engage in normal, innocent risk-taking behavior—as boys will do—we get caught in a protective net of community vigilance. Thus, we learn another lesson about society's leeriness of black males. We learn either to be cautious if not timid in our public actions, or to throw caution to the wind as we proclaim our presence on the public stage.

What is it about being black and male that causes our parents to encourage such vigilance? As we struggle to understand ourselves, we ask ourselves, why is avoiding trouble so serious for us, and a mother's prime worry? Children often follow their parents' advice with little understanding of what lies beneath. The young accept on faith. But our parents make caution an imperative. It is embedded in their conversation and coded communication with other family members. It can be the casual topic of dinner conversation, or hinted at in the breakfast instructions of do's and don'ts before going to school.

We pick the same message up from the men on the street: "Wait 'til you become a man, little brother." Through their message we become aware of that life marker, that milestone called manhood, the inevitable point that separates our boyhood innocence from adult reality. Via those men on our street corners, deeper meanings are given to our mothers' admonitions. We intuitively sense that manhood is a boundary, and that once it is crossed the stakes will be higher because the risks to our welfare increase. Very often we plunge into whatever we think manhood is to allay our mothers' worries about our safety, rather than to reach true adult responsibility.

How Shattered Dreams Start Changing Our Outlook

James slouched on the couch next to me as his parents' voices conveyed their perplexity and exasperation about their thirteen-year-old son's behavior. His transgressions were many: He had been cited for truancy, his grades were poor, he was lazy and had to be made to do his chores around the home, and he was always fighting with his fifteen-year-old sister. "In sum, he has a bad attitude," said his father, "and he needs an ass whipping—which his mother won't let me give him." James cut his eyes, looking provocatively at his father, who was held in check by his mother—who admits to keeping peace between the two of them.

James's behavior was once exemplary. He had attended a small public elementary school in his neighborhood, where he excelled; now he attended a larger middle school that had fewer resources, a poor performance record, and significant discipline problems. The vast majority of the students were African Americans. Only a few of its graduates were tracked to the competitive high schools. James was quite clear about this. He saw his parents as helpless to change his school because of where they lived. They could not afford to move.

Due to gang activity, the police were a constant presence. James felt the white police officers provoked conflict with their intimidating attitudes. He was lumped with all black males, as far as the authorities were concerned—stamped with "guilty before proven innocent," as James put it. He had been to juvenile court once for an incident he claims he had nothing to do with. Like many young black men, James knew that black juveniles are far more likely than white youth to be dealt harsh treatment in the juvenile justice system.

James also had to deal with the reality of what his parents could and could not do for the family. It was stressful, and he felt trapped (a feeling his father often spoke of having when *he* was a youth) and angry about not being able to change his situation. His childhood dreams of becoming an astronaut were shattered, a disclosure that surfaced only by accident, since it had become so unobtainable and buried in his mind.

Becoming One of the Boys: A Matter of Survival

By watching the men and older boys in our neighborhoods playing cards, chess, dominoes, or checkers, listening to the banter in their verbal give-and-take, the acceptance and brokering of interpersonal limits that define friendship, we hear about rules for survival within these circles of friendship. At these moments we learn what hanging out and drinking means, how closeness develops. We learn how to play and be a player, guarding our disclosures, vigilant about trustworthiness, but trusting nevertheless. It is a singular fraternity that young black boys learn can be joined only through making the journey across the burning sands of adolescence. Only then are we accepted into the brotherhood. We come to understand what's happening in the community by what happens to *us* in the community.

To grow up as an African American male child is to learn you are special—prized in some quarters and hated in others. We learn we are unique by the attention we attract, and we learn we attract unique attention. Listening to the experiences of other black men and contending with the attention we attract when we are with our buddies puts these experiences into perspective and helps to convey strategies for dealing with invisibility.

Thus, the "distinct walk," the ability to rap and communicate as only "brothers" do, our distinguishing dress styles, athletic prowess, an unsubmissive, noncommittal but highly sexualized attitude toward black girls, a guarded but highly prized trust between each other, a fratricidal vengeance when personal violations occur, all contribute to what shapes black male identity. These are the foundational experiences and therefore the platform upon which we must struggle with the paradox of being visible one moment—for example, through the suspicion raised by our gathering in groups—and invisible the next, such as when our complaints about the treatment of us when we are in groups is dismissed. There are ground rules we must learn quickly in order to survive the paradox of being seen but not seen, because we will be treated differently as adults.

But it is often difficult for young boys to sort out all these experiences and to maneuver their lives in directions that serve their best interests. We latch onto survival guidelines—a subset of the brotherhood rules I discussed earlier—such as "copping" an attitude at the right time. We find comfort behind the protective shield provided by our unique camaraderie, the feeling that we are young men soon to be adults, resonating an unspoken deep allegiance to stick together, particularly in difficult times, particularly when our dignity is under attack. At this time we expect allegiance to the value of the brotherhood: "I got your back, you got mine." In part because we have survived our childhood, we now know how to scrutinize people and places that honor the dignity we have earned among each other. We now know some of the reactions to us as young men, and some of the ways to handle them.

Therefore, it should not have been surprising to see so many black adolescents attend the Million Man March in Washington, D.C., despite the media's preoccupation with the Minister Louis Farrakhan and who he represented. The march was an expression of a deeply shared understanding about the weight of being a black man in America. The convener, Minister Farrakhan, was only an instrument of that shared understanding, otherwise there would not have been such an assembly or outpouring of fraternal closeness on that special sunny day.

Watching Models of Conflict, Sacrifice, and Pride

Most poignantly, we see our parents and other adults around us as role models who go through their own personal encounters with racism, and we develop our own understanding of what that means for them. Their experiences inevitably alert us to the fact that we are members of a very special ethnic group. They show that as boys, and ultimately as adult men, we will have different challenges than do black women.

Sam's father (a silent and gentle man) left the family after years of being in and out of the home. Sam had a strong attachment to him. He knew his father had struggled in life. He later came to understand from both his mother and from learning more about his father that this struggle was related to his father's unwillingness to be stuck in dead-end jobs that offered no future.

His mother only hinted at the depths of his father's struggle by saying his personality made it difficult for him to accept certain things. Drinking heavily, relatives said, was one of the ways his father quelled feelings of anger and despondency about not being able to provide more for his family. Sam's mother told him that his father was deeply angered and frustrated by the inequities produced by racism. He saw his real self as quite different from what his life circumstances represented. Nevertheless, what Sam always remembers is that whenever his father came around he was always sober and dressed in fine, stylish clothes.

His father was proper in the way he spoke. He seemed to be a font of knowledge about almost any subject, very well-read, with an extremely engaging personality. He talked with all the children about staying in school, reading, and acquiring knowledge. "Knowledge is power" was his motto. He emphasized repeatedly that they should obey their mother, and gave clear warnings about what he might do if he heard otherwise. He taught them the importance of dressing well, "because your clothes, how good you look, and how you carry yourself, tell people who you are." Sam thought his father was one of the most decent men alive.

Sam's absent father was reincarnated as a "ghost" in the day-to-day activities of his family. As an adult, Sam understood his father's circumstances, but as a young boy, his father was like an apparition to Sam: You could sense his presence in the thoughts and feelings of his mother, brother, and sisters, though he was not physically in the house. When his mother disciplined them, behind her warnings was frequently an unspoken "This is what your father would also expect of you children." By invoking his presence (as she also did with God), Sam felt his mother believed she gained added parental authority.

As a child, Sam could not understand how his father, who was so intelligent, was not more successful. According to family members, his father, in spite of his obvious high I.Q., was not admitted into a number of high-level schools and was frequently denied job opportunities for which he was well qualified. Disappointed and angered by tokenism, he dropped out of school and subsequently gave up trying for special opportunities. Instead, he focused his energy on supporting the education of his younger brothers and sisters. Sam's father knew that such a sacrifice meant a trade-off of education for job security. After a while, job seniority became more important in his supporting of his family. However, as a self-educated man it was intolerable to him to have his superior knowledge belittled by being placed in inferior positions and receiving stereotypical treatment. His underlying, seething anger caused him to quit job after job when he thought supervisors were treating him unfairly because he was black. This compromised his desire to gain seniority and thus job security.

In his father's life, Sam sees a story about denied opportunities and sacrifice, but it is also a story about protecting one's self-respect despite circumstances. Sam's father found a way of maintaining civility and decency in spite of how his experiences of inequities tested him. Sam learned from his father a way of being visible in spite of how others will try to pigeonhole you.

There are many of us who, no matter how sick we are, will always try to look good, or at least better than we feel. Within that need to look good, regardless of our illness, is the will to live, which is our capacity to be resilient. Sam learned from his father's behavior the importance of pride in being who you are.

Learning about Dignity

As a child, Bill learned from his father to "not take any mess from anybody." That was a family rule handed down from his grandfather to his father. His maternal aunts and uncles and his father's brothers and sisters also lived up to the family credo. Family conversations were often centered on how one family member or another had handled racist encounters and maintained his or her dignity. Moreover, it was family custom to consult or involve other family members if you had doubts about how to handle any racially tinged situation. "Don't ever feel you have to go it alone" was a family mantra.

One example of this was the family's collective efforts to help Bill's uncle fight an unfair attempt by a county government in the south to take over his property. The family pooled their resources and won the battle.

Bill still remembers being "mortified" in his sixth-grade classroom when his mother visited his school to discuss the lack of African American literature in his teacher's assignments. "The consolation," noted Bill, "was that my father had to work and couldn't come along—thank God!"

"My parents are a piece of work—a dynamic duo—when it comes to race matters. You have no idea what it's like to grow up with two parents hell-bent on proper recognition and treatment," Bill said with a slight smile. It was his awareness of these family practices and values that largely produced Bill's discomfort with how he handled himself at the restaurant. Thus, his outburst of rage at the taxi driver was his way—at that moment—of affirming another family maxim, "You have to stand up and be counted for the race."

Relatives would look his way and admonish him to not forget to protect the family name. As a young child, however, and still somewhat as an adult, Bill was reluctant to address racial indignities head-on. But how he handled them was consequential for his stature within the family.

This sense of racial responsibility caused Bill to feel a deep sense of burden, because of having to spend a lifetime literally fighting racism. It was a demanding and stressful responsibility.

Racial Identity Parenting: How Instructions on How to Be a Black Man Can Create Dilemmas

Racial-identity parenting influences not only our outlook on life, our outlook as people of African descent, but also our identity as men.

I asked Carlos, a dark-skinned sixteen-year-old, about his struggle in a troublesome school. He said it was difficult for him and his friends because of their skin color, but he agreed with his mother that the black kids brought it on themselves by exclusively hanging together. In probing his views, it became apparent that Carlos felt it important to be known as just an American, and that his upbringing had no emphasis on being black or discussing black issues—except for the belief that acting like black kids is what holds you back.

Karim, on the other hand, was a fifteen-year-old fair-skinned young man who wore African attire and adornments and spoke knowledgeably about black issues. His father and he were enrolled in an African drum and dance troupe as a shared father-son activity. The family was immersed in many activities that were African-centered, and they were conversant with the political and social issues of people of African descent.

Justin, a sixteen-year-old brown-skinned young man, was one of the organizers of his school's multicultural day. He spoke to the gathering about the issues of people of African descent and the necessity to build bridges of understanding between ethnic groups. When I spoke with him further, he disclosed how both his mother and father were leaders in similar ways at their jobs and in the community.

Our families vary in their lessons about leading lives as black men. Some are more direct, some are indirect, and others are neglectful in providing instructions on how to be, and how to be seen in the world, as young men of African descent. While the lessons we take away help establish within us standards for recognition and feelings of legitimacy, and determine our criteria for respect and dignity, there's a catch. If we waver in our racial identity, or in our identity as men, we become vulnerable to the various pulls into invisibility—such as denying ancestry—that permeate American culture. When a boy has chameleon-like identities that change with circumstances, it's a sign that invisibility is an issue in his life.

Children pick up unpredictable innuendoes from their parents' struggles. For example, Joe's father, frequently angry over conditions on his job, thought keeping it was preferable to his own father's tendency to work odd jobs while trying to build an ever-elusive business. The discontent and unfulfilled dreams from staying at the same job for security's sake made him withdraw into himself. This sacrifice for his family—enduring bigotry on the job in order to make a living—was costly to how he felt as a man.

As a child, Joe resented the time his father spent discussing "the plight of the black man" with his buddies. Watching his father struggle with these "demons" in order to support the family shaped Joe's reluctance to commit to a relationship. But no matter what his opinion of his father's circumstances, he knew his father put up with a lot in order to bring home a paycheck and take care of his family. He and Joe's mom did not compromise on supporting the family, even if it meant suffering racial indignities. They did what they had to do together. Joe could not see how to fulfill his dreams, carrying those particular burdens of family. His mother and father always told him that you cannot achieve dreams without the responsibility that comes with them.

Joe has worked to preserve their dignity. Each in his or her own way expressed concerns about race to him. They each taught him how to maintain legitimacy in the face of indignities. He learned from his father to be visible by embodying certain values about being a man. In different ways, their presence was felt and internalized as special. Joe grew to know what motivated his father's behavior as a black man, and thus learned what to anticipate in the future as an adult. But Joe still absorbed his father's sense of invisibility.

Learning about Intimacy and Love

Boys are sensitive but not all-knowing. Sam was an adult before he fully understood why his mother called upon his father's disciplinarian image. It was a way to keep him involved in the family, even in absentia. She loved her husband. She understood his anger and pain but felt helpless to solve it. She understood his coming and going as a matter of his maintaining self-respect, until they finally both agreed that it was causing harm to the children and that it was best to separate. His being able to provide was how he defined being a father. Not fulfilling these responsibilities to his satisfaction was frustrating and humiliating.

As a child, Sam noted that his father resisted the pressures at work to be "something other folks imagine I am, or would like me to be, just to make them comfortable." I consider this an illustration of a person's will to fight off the viral infection of invisibility. In other words, one must resist pressures to conform to what racism defines for a black man as tolerable behavior, in order to be partially included in the larger society. But Sam was too young to know that it was difficult, if not impossible, to acquire an inner satisfaction in a partnership when your self-respect and dignity as a man are threatened by the way society treats you. His childhood was filled with the irrationality of prejudice, but he did not fully comprehend its influence on the relationship between his mother and father. They each contended with confusion and disillusionment. At this tender age, Sam could not see his father's bitter struggle for dignity and respect, but instead saw a peculiar character trait that left him uncertain about what to think of his father, even while continuing to love him. These experiences set the psychological backdrop for the way Sam would meet his own intimacy challenges as a black man. The die was being cast. The struggle that began on the playground and at home would continue in his primary school years and beyond.

Schools as Cultivators of Invisibility

"Being in special education classes was a badge of distinction, a cut above time in jail," Sam remarked with a chuckle. "All of us brothers would compare strategies on how to get over, sharing with each other what to do to remain in special placement. It was like a fraternity and a fool's paradise. We got satisfaction from being together when our being together was a sign that school had given up on us; but we were too naïve to know what we were being slated for."

In their efforts to make school meaningful, Sam and his fellow classmates became master manipulators. Their classes required little schoolwork, so it gave them time to concentrate on their schemes to have their own way in their classrooms, during recess, on the corner in their neighborhood, or working the women—or, in other words, being somebody on their own terms. "It was not about science and math, it was about being brothers in charge." They took pride in their abilities to make things happen, and they received recognition, even if it was from teachers and other authorities who found their behavior unacceptable. Causing chaos in school made them feel that they had control of their school experiences. They usurped considerable power to make things happen for themselves by drawing the attention of school authorities on a daily basis. The satisfaction they could not acquire from classroom work they found in their created activities. It meaningfully filled a day.

An environment where there exists little positive acknowledgment, few rewards, and hardly any sense of belonging or acceptance breeds the invisibility syndrome. What parents and teachers present as the purpose of school was nothing like what Sam experienced. In fact, Sam felt lost and insignificant in classroom activities. He did not believe that he would fulfill his parents' expectations, because there was nothing in his daily school activities that made him feel that he could. Education, as a path toward upward mobility, was his mother's dream. The unfortunate truth is that Sam was not encouraged by a school of predominantly white teachers to make his education a stepping-stone to a future career, but rather that it was an activity he was supposed to fill his day with until it was time to go home. He therefore saw no reason to apply himself.

The Fourth-Grade Syndrome

The foundation is laid early for what eventually becomes the "fourth-grade syndrome," where so many African American boys begin a precipitous decline in academic performance—a decline fostered by attitudes that say "they are not going to amount to much" when referring to African American boys. In his book, *Family Life and School Achievement: Why Poor Black Children Succeed or Fail,* educational researcher Reginald Clarke reports how the amount of time spent in class academic activities is crucial to success. It is as important for teachers to work with students as it is for students to work on lessons, both in class and at home. Educators have known for a long time that student performance is closely related to teacher expectations. Low expectations beget low performance. High expectations result in high performance.

Many young men of African descent can look back over several generations and see that this did *not* happen. It is simply amazing how many African American boys feel that securing an education means overcoming nonsupportive teachers and school climates that expect them to fail. They feel that there are no good reasons for their participation in school. Participation seems irrelevant to their daily life and their future as young black men. The promises of education are very often more connected to hope than reality. This is widely reflected by the disillusionment among black teens in many inner-city school systems.

Black Invisibility in the School Curriculum

Sam remembers what he calls the "out-of-the-drawer" Black History Month. "Every February, our history came out of the teacher's desk, and every March it went back in. They put up these black faces on posters and tell us we ought to be proud of how they won our civil rights. These are our role models, they would say. For what, I would say? They hadn't changed my life. No one connected the dots.

"I thought, if Mama's education sermon was so true, how come being a civil rights leader was the only job available? No black person ever seemed to discover anything, and it seemed that we ourselves were never discovered until February."

A primary psychological shaper of the invisibility syndrome is how people of African descent are represented in the school curriculum. Moreover, many teachers are uninformed about African and African American history, and many are not personally invested in its instruction, other than in obligatory school lesson plans. The greater emphasis on African American history and culture during February, and its sporadic emphasis throughout the rest of the school year, inevitably conveys insignificance and, at best, is tangential to guiding boys' dreams into becoming reality.

The truncated curriculum does not inspire or motivate in ways that a fully integrated history, of African peoples can to validate the individual. Therefore, the ideal goal set for Black History Month often is not achieved. This seasonal appearance, this half-hearted exposition of our history, reinforces invisibility by making students feel that the contributions of people of African descent are fleeting, frequently troubled episodes of history, rather than an integral part of its totality. This engenders psychological marginality and also lessens the importance attached to being of African descent.

Learning continuously how previous generations of African American men ("role models") contributed in constructive and diverse ways to the world provides acknowledgment and inner satisfaction, as well as an appreciation for one's gender and race that can build self-pride in children of African descent. It develops group identity and a sense of belonging, i.e., an internalization of self-worth and legitimacy.

Learning that men of African descent have made significant contributions to society would validate our feelings of worth and self-respect. Educators who make these messages day-to-day, year-to-year classroom experiences for us give us a different sense of how to be visible with dignity.

Invisibility's Linkage to Our Childhood Dreams

In New York, a principal asked a ten-year-old African American boy what he wanted to be. He indicated interest in going to law school and then becoming a judge. With contemptuous disbelief, she asked him what made him think he could get into law school, and who would come to *him* as a judge. His friend, standing nearby, spoke up and said that *he* would come to his friend. A contentious and animated discussion followed between the principal and the two students. The principal was put off by the boys' willingness to assert their positions, and—interpreting it as insubordination—she suspended them for two days. It took their parents' indignation to allow the boys to return to school.

This type of incident, where a young man's future is prejudged by negative attitudes, is common for African American boys. Many of us experience some form of this attitude during our school years. We find many people discounting our ability to amount to very much—and it even becomes reflected in what they say and do on our behalf. Behavior like the principal's works to snuff out dreams through belittling our aspirations, but it also pushes us to the background by its lack of support. It conveys a message that we are insignificant when outside of a designated box filled with negative attitudes and stereotypes. It says we must remain within society's four walls of narrow expectations and stay only in the world created by our own community—often isolated and alone, cut off from the real resources that can help us fulfill our aspirations. Thus, invisibility takes a firmer hold in the unconscious mind and bores the message of worthlessness a little deeper.

Our school environment often connects our dreams to futile expectations of the future. The reality of school life is too often unrelated to our parents' educational mission for us. Black boys and men are not expected to be included. This cultivates alienation and ambivalence toward formal education. It forces us to focus on the peer group as a means of salvaging our self-esteem both in and out of the classroom.

The lack of relevance to our reality makes the logic of attending school perplexing at best. What schools often provide for boys of African descent is a slowly nurtured understanding that being somebody is more directly attached to the peer culture than to the classroom culture. Our potential and ability are robbed by the climate in schools thoughtlessly. It moves the criteria for acceptable visibility away from being smart to being social, for it is in the social milieu that you gain meaningful recognition and legitimacy—hence a redefined visibility. Such attitudes cultivated among black males by the school environment play into racially coded expectations that become a self-fulfilling prophecy. Poorly equipped schools, school environments preoccupied with behavior problems, mismatches between acquired, marketable skills and career opportunities, and the resulting awareness of our increasing marginality as young adults—all contribute to the way society makes African American men invisible and undermines their interest in learning. Many young boys of African descent fight a loss of faith, feeling that the outcome of education is not worth the humiliation.

Finding Validation—Trey's Story

"Look at what you can do if you study," Trey, a fourteen-year-old boy, said, mimicking his mother's predictable remark when any white kid's accomplishment was paraded on TV or in the newspapers. The accomplishments of kids of African descent were rarely seen in the public media, but Trey knew that his mother's intentions were sincere. She used anything to motivate him. But she was unaware of how much he resented her references to the achievements of white kids. He did not want his mother to use them as a standard for him. "I have nothing in common with them," he frequently told me. Trey did not want to upset his mother, so he kept these feelings to himself.

I would learn, as Trey disclosed his feelings, that not seeing or hearing about accomplishments of men of African descent had a powerful impact on him. He had internalized his efforts to meet his mother's standards of achievement as lonely endeavors. Schoolwork bore little relevance to his daily life out on the streets; in it he saw no connection to his future, given the lack of black men that *he* knew of reaping the rewards of any of the opportunities his mother encouraged him to pursue. When he couldn't see the payoff, he couldn't see why he should make so much effort to study.

Despite his mother's passionate belief that a good education greatly improved the quality of one's life, Trey had had classroom experiences that challenged his mother's dreams for him. They also began to transform his view of opportunity and success. For example, Trey already had numerous experiences of having his raised hand ignored by white teachers, or his clearly accurate answers treated as inadequate. Those classroom experiences cultivated frustration and a deep suspicion about the teachers' genuine interest in him. The white teachers lost credibility as genuine educators in Trey's eyes because they had no expectations of his succeeding. These types of classroom incidents transformed his criteria for belonging in school. He began to look elsewhere for validation. Trey lost his original positive attitude about the value of school and moved to street life for his recognition and acceptance. In street life he had authority and a reputation.

Choosing to Be Smart or Dumb—Straddling Two Worlds

"I don't know if I can go through with this," said seventeen-year-old Chris, with growing conviction. I noted that his family was counting on his graduating from prep school and being excited about his admission to Harvard. "It's not right," he kept repeating. "My partners didn't get the same opportunity as me. Many have been in and out of jail and seem not to be going anywhere. But they keep rooting for me. It's crazy—just luck that I'm here." I reminded Chris of his late mother's fight for his education. She had fought every teacher and administrator who doubted Chris's ability, finally getting him into special after-school and summer programs preparing middle school students for entry into private schools. Chris excelled, but now he felt guilty. He saw the chasm growing between his different lifestyle and that of his friends from the old neighborhood. These were experiences he could not reconcile. He felt special and accepted by his friends.

His late mother's best friend, and now his guardian, had pledged to fulfill her dreams for her son. Chris had failures in his last terms in school because he was fearful of losing his identity as a brother and a young black man. He saw this new opportunity as threatening, and he was uncertain that he liked what he was becoming. There was little that affirmed his life as a young man of African descent. He didn't know if he liked being an educated and learned black man, if this opportunity sacrificed the life he knew. For him, it raised questions of allegiance to friends who had not had his opportunities, and it confused him about how to represent himself to them. It also raised fears about the un-charted waters that come with new opportunities.

His friends had defended his being gifted and smart when school-mates challenged him for being committed to his studies. Many of his schoolmates experienced school differently, and they poked fun at his academic success. It was confusing for him, and he had no one to talk to about his feelings. He began to sabotage his late mother's dream and his own desires, for fear of losing himself to a way of life that had ap-peal, but no relevance to those who mattered most to him—his part-ners, the brothers who supported and rooted for him in spite of his own misgivings.

Chris's impending struggle with straddling two worlds—one that was where many of his friends were, and the other, a predominately white world, that was where his friends were not—is another manifes-tation of DuBois's double consciousness, "two warring souls" within black people. Chris worried about leaving the personal comfort zone among his friends that gave him a special kind of visibility as a person.

He could not rely upon new acquaintances for support in a community he had little experience with. Moreover, the price for taking full advantage of this opportunity to Chris meant abandoning old ties. In his young mind the price was too high. His childhood and adolescent experiences of being accepted outside of his community made him reluctant to pay the dues. The way Chris saw himself would be lost to the way a new career, a new way of life, would define his visibility. Now he was torn between his late mother's dream and his own emerging values of preserving personal dignity as a black man. Holding on to his black identity would be a challenge in settings where it was not valued.

Chris's dilemma represents a typical conflict between the classic hope for upward mobility through education instilled by mothers and fathers, and the personal sacrifices and costs required to get that good education. From early in our childhood we learn that education is a means of getting out of poverty or elevating our social and economic status, but there is also a not-so-veiled hope that the mantle of education will rid us of the black male stigma we are endowed with by society's attitudes. There are implicit guidelines for who and what makes us feel legitimate. To whom do we look for validation of what we experience, the checking of our sanity, as education provides new opportunities and associates? What do we accept as acknowledgment of our achievement, if new opportunities ignore or even disrespect our heritage? How does our new opportunity complement or merge with our identity as men of African descent, if our acceptance of that identity is problematic? Without there being a positive affirmation of our being men of African descent in our new opportunities, that part of our identity becomes marginalized and thus devalued.

For Chris and many black male teenagers, to accept opportunities with new acquaintances and new experiences also means having to evaluate how consistent they are with the way they want to be visible as young African American men. When experiences within new opportunities devalue your identity as African American men, then choosing opportunities that implicitly support such notions or practices in effect puts you in the position of devaluing yourself. If becoming smart and educated means the corruption of racial identity, it gives credence to sentiments that say you have sold out. On one of those levels, you become invisible.

Creating Places of Visibility: The Problem of Limited Arenas for Experiencing Personal Power

It is not difficult for us as boys to learn that unrewarding school experiences lead us nowhere; whereas, what we are able to create with our peers are more fulfilling experiences and lead somewhere. The feeling that "school is not the place for me" is quickly imprinted.

To compensate, we make our own rewarding school experiences that build self-esteem, or what I call "create our places of visibility." Friends are essential to help create and sustain these contexts of visibility. They are important in creating the social milieu that defies conventional expectations of school behavior, goals, and objectives. They are partners in a peer group enterprise to make schools bearable.

Schools can unwittingly collude in this enterprise. For example, the importance schools attach to athletics provides a context of visibility. Very often, we feel that this is the only place school truly promotes us for special acknowledgment, rewards, legitimacy, and validation. Coming out of our participation and our demonstration of talents and skills is an ensemble of rewards. We have certified visibility as part of the athletic program. Both peer groups and school expectations support our excelling in this area.

This endorsement has broad support, bestowing high status. We easily find arenas for our talents, special camaraderie among teammates, adoration from other males, and attractiveness to females that validates one's efforts. Consequently, there is a powerful inclusiveness derived from success in an athletic program for African American males. The recognition gained in this place of visibility bestows a kind of mainstream identity and a validation that is not experienced by being an accomplished student. However, the privileges gained by the African American athlete are primarily tied to physical success in sports. To be an athlete garners a special type of recognition; but we are not seen as real people with differentiated needs that go beyond the athlete's persona. In fact, as people we are not seen at all—we are still invisible. Like the gladiators of old, we are no more than our designated roles: entertainers.

Learning to Survive No Matter the Place

As Sam grew up in the "hood" and learned that his mother's advice alone would not keep him alive, he joined one of the gangs, loosely formed cliques that one had to be associated with in order to walk the streets without repeated challenges. This was his community. Racism created it and poverty perpetuated it. This is where he had to carve out his identity.

Sam became a problem child, frequently getting in trouble in school or in the neighborhood. He taunted his teachers and the police with an intimidating attitude whenever he felt they disrespected him. His difficult behavior resulted in his placement in special education classes. He was diagnosed as being hyperactive, along with other inferred learning disabilities. "That meant I wasn't good at staying in my seat or concentrating on my work. The teachers had a code of silence for what they were *not* doing in the classroom, versus their claims of what they were unable to do with me in the classroom." Sam says his placement was a joke. His recollection was that he was actually active—bouncing off the walls because of boredom, feeling trapped, and believing that no one—especially he—could make sense of the uselessness of those classroom activities.

"Looking back, I took those tests they convinced my mother I needed without caring—just gave any answer. And they didn't seem to worry whether I was doing it right or wrong. They took the answers I gave as genuine. I just wanted to get the test over with. But I think my performance confirmed their beliefs about me, making my answers seem believable."

I asked Sam to describe how he was feeling during this period. Unable to fully describe his feelings, Sam noted that they were many and mixed, depending upon the day. Many times he felt overwhelmed by the drama of life around him as a child, but he couldn't let on how much it bothered him. "A lot was going on at home, a lot was going on in the streets—and a lot damn sure *wasn't* going on in the classroom. I was trapped by the limitations of my poor neighborhood, and I felt it defining me."

Learning Self-Reliance on the Streets

The task of growing up as young black men in the inner city is largely a matter of being resilient. In order to survive, many of us developed strong skills of self-reliance, because depending upon others is so conditional and transient. Mothers and fathers cannot help you when you're alone on the streets. Self-reliance therefore becomes an important survival skill. It is corrupted by the limited resources that we compete for in our neighborhoods, which in turn corrupts our understanding of competitiveness.

Sylvester Monroe and Peter Goldman's book *Brothers* powerfully illustrates how choices in an urban housing project achieved visibility for Monroe's best friend, "Half Man," who talks about his life in the third person. Half Man had more than other youngsters in the projects. He successfully worked the various hustles, while the other young brothers struggled and were penniless. There was great complexity to Half Man's approach to life, yet, he never left home. Viewing life in the present tense in anticipation of the future, Monroe noted that:

> When people say that guys like Half Man don't have any sense of the future, it's not that clear cut. The future they see is shut off. It's closed. You're afraid to dream for fear of not reaching it, so you don't set up any goals, and that way you don't fail. You just live for now. You get as much as you can today.

Sam and his childhood friends were very much in awe of the brothers who seemed to have found a distinctive street presence. It was alluring, it held power, and it bestowed a form of dignity and respect. Other brothers would seek their counsel, and sisters would want to be with them because of their status. Having a hustle that provided more money than others had further propped up their identity and thus became a necessity.

But Sam sensed there was something hollow about it all. The lure was part of a trap to make more of this type of stature than it was worth. The "cool" brothers set standards for others, and there was power and respect in this ability. They had the clothes, jewelry, cars, and electronic gadgets. They threw the parties and knew how to get the women. They were somebody.

But there was also a desperation born of frustration that guided their behavior—unspoken fears, unknown indignation buried deep within an inner emotional world that Sam and his partners covered with a layer of apparent self-reliance. It is this façade of self-reliance that we carry into adult life, hiding the frustration and anger about our circumstances, the struggle with society's unwillingness to fully include us, and our own sense of powerlessness to bring about change. Childhood teaches us strange lessons about becoming adult men of African descent.

6

Becoming Our Fathers

There are no roadmaps for black fatherhood, much less manhood. Most men piece it together based on what they observe growing up, and hope it will work. For most of my friends, it was on-the-job training. In hindsight, we were fortunate. Our relatives and friends never failed to let us know how well we were doing, and many of us had fathers around, or surrogate fathers on whom we could model our manhood. Older brothers, grandfathers, uncles, close male friends of the family, church members, and neighbors all kept a watchful eye when we were just beyond our mothers' reach. They shadowed our mothers' rearing as they subtly communicated to us that as men there was something else out there that only they, not Mom, knew was waiting for us.

We learned from these men that bringing home the paycheck was what being a man was all about. Real men worked enough hours and at enough jobs to provide for and gain the respect of family and friends.

However, another significant message was communicated to the boys and young men of my generation. We heard it in loud voices and in low undertones, saw it in stooped shoulders and indifferent shrugs. We detected it verbally and nonverbally. It seeped into our consciousness and unconsciousness, so that by adulthood we knew, without a doubt: It was and is profoundly difficult for black men to be successful providers.

Our Work—The Imperative to Be Good at Something

Work, and being successful at it, is closely tied to how we feel about ourselves and how we believe others should feel about us. It is linked to our dignity and self-respect. Our jobs, careers, employment, are all primary sources of recognition and acknowledgment as men, as fathers, and as family men.

Getting a "good" job and doing it well fortifies us. With a good job, we are able to carry out more supportive, nurturing activities with our children. Success at work—being a provider—secures our sense of manhood and allows us to perform freely and comfortably as fathers. If we have no job, no means of generating income for the family, then who are we as men? Ever since the Emancipation, the work African American men performed—whether in the fields, the "big house," the skilled trades, in business, or whatever "hustle"—determined our credibility.

Success at what we consider as "our work" is a way of demonstrating that we have our life under control, despite the indignities we face as African American men. In keeping with the long legacy of men of African descent, our code, often on an unconscious level, demands that we create something that we are "good at." Not one of us wishes to think we are victims of our race and gender. So we explore and invent many avenues to make things happen in our lives that become "our work," that make us proud, giving us a source of dignity and self-respect. Drug trafficking, or finding that perfect hustle, not excepted.

If You've Got a Good Job, You'd Better Keep It

A friend's grandfather—the man who raised him—worked in maintenance at a garment factory in New York and ran the old-style elevators that required manual operators for thirty years. Cyril Smalls, or "Pops," worked six days a week, taking on a few side jobs for extra money from time to time, and rested only on his day of worship. His wife did not have to work, although she did so to augment the family income. He went to work in a shirt and tie every day, changed into his coveralls, and required everyone in his workplace to address him as Mr. Smalls. It was during the Great Depression that he got his job, and he would quite often say to us boys, "If you get a good job, you better keep it."

Another friend's father worked many jobs, primarily as a sales representative. Although smart, articulate, and engagingly confident, he had no chance of getting a promotion. For a black man to get promoted to supervisor or manager level was unheard of in those days. The ceiling was not glass, it was made of brick and mortar. But still he provided for his family. Despite these indignities, some whispered that he had privileges because his skin was fair.

Indeed, there were light-skinned African American men in my extended family, the neighborhood, and the church whose employment was directly related to their fairness. We all knew the rule: If by chance we bumped into them while at work we were not to show any recognition, for fear of exposing their "passing." To do so could jeopardize their jobs. We African Americans have always had criteria for acceptable and unacceptable ways of presenting ourselves for work and keeping our dignity—from employment in the "big house" to Affirmative Action.

Our code is that men do what they have to do in order to survive and provide, as they always have and as they always will. The question becomes, at what price to our dignity and self-respect, and at what price to feel and act like the fathers we want to be?

As I said earlier, many of us have learned, with or without our fathers around, that to get ahead you have to work "day and night." That message is also coupled with implicit and explicit messages that we should be prepared, as African American men, to work twice as hard and be twice as good. The combination of our race and our gender puts us at risk of not getting that "good job," and it can also be a factor in our ability to keep it. This has significant implications for our children.

The Difficulty of Demonstrating Personal Power

Our belief about how to be a father in part determines the destinies of our sons and daughters. What does it mean if we define a "strong and caring" father as one who provides money for food and shelter? What if success at this becomes the only way to feel that we have fulfilled our responsibility?

If our paternal self-image and dreams cannot remain clear to us in the face of humiliation, frequent loss of employment, or little upward mobility in our job, the invisibility virus within us grows strong. This awareness brings about feelings of vulnerability, shakes our sense of being strong fathers upon whose shoulders our children can stand, and weakens our sense of manhood. Remember, this is what Joe felt about his father's commitment to a job filled with inequities. He vowed not to follow in his father's footsteps, or embrace his concept of hard work if it meant being subjected to humiliation. If "strong" means that you are not intimidated, can "face down" adversity, and can protect the welfare of your children, then being defiant when your job status is threatened elevates your stature in the eyes of your sons and daughters, to whom you wish to appear "powerful," no matter what.

The Difficulty of Regrouping from Humiliation— John's Story

John was driving home with his family following a long weekend vacation when the police stopped him. John was forcibly yanked from the car and spread-eagled over the hood, with his face pushed down and the barrel of a gun jammed into his neck. In this demeaning position he muttered, "There must be a mistake." Upon noticing his young son peering at him through the windshield with bewildered, frightened, teary eyes, John almost threw caution to the wind. Flashing through his mind were numerous thoughts about how to instantly handle this unpleasant situation. He wanted to wrest himself free, stand up tall, and look the officers in the eyes, declaring they made a mistake. He wanted to act in defiance of his mistreatment for his son's eyes. But such justified defiance would have been interpreted as resistance by the police officers, and would have given them reason to further mishandle him under the guise of self-protection. Thinking of his family in the car, John capped his impulses in order to defuse the situation and prevent his being taken to jail unnecessarily. Satisfied that he was not their suspect, the cops released him and left with no apologies. John was left to reenter his car and face his son.

A major challenge for John upon reentering that car, as it is for all African American men regrouping from humiliating, racist-driven situations, is to react in ways that show his children and his wife how he maintains his self-respect and dignity after such an episode.

Many of us first get angry and vengeful in our thinking. It is hard not to, given the brutal history of the treatment of African American men. Even when we think our education and elevated social status should exempt us from such incidents, we are pulled right back into the category of "all black men" when they happen, thrown into another encounter with invisibility.

A friend was driving his elderly father-in-law to speak at a church one day when he lost his way. They slowed down while trying to find their location, and a white male motorist traveling behind them became annoyed, then began tailgating and honking his horn. When he finally managed to pull around them he shouted racially provocative comments and gestures as he passed. My friend's father-in-law firmly fixed the motorist in his eyes and said with exaggerated articulation but genuine sincerity, "God bless you, my son." Both my friend and his father-in-law are Christian ministers. My friend was not as forgiving, and he found himself learning yet another valuable lesson from his father-in-law about the power of forgiving and controlling impulses when racially provoked. That many of us could be so forgiving under the circumstances is doubtful.

As fathers, we can explain these episodes with John and my friend's father-in-law to our sons as the blows you must absorb as a black man in racist America. Or, for some fathers, it may be simpler to try to minimize the effects by teaching children to ignore them. If we can be treated this way in public, then how do we handle and report to loved ones those more personal, private affronts where only our conscience is the judge of our behavior?

The Dilemma of Expressing Genuine Interest— Earl's Story

During one of our therapy sessions, my patient Earl, a construction worker, talked about going to his son Bobby's school alone one evening for a routine parent-teachers' conference. He came away feeling like a persona non grata, treated like the Creature from the Black Lagoon, although he had visited the school many times before with his wife. School guards and administrators acted cautious and suspicious as he walked the halls looking for Bobby's homeroom. He was frequently stopped and asked where he was going and what he wanted.

Contrasting sharply to what he saw happening to the mothers, Earl was not received as a concerned father. It appeared that the school officials were prepared to meet with mothers but not fathers, and most certainly not black fathers. This unfriendly reception left him wondering, "If this is the way I am treated, how are they treating my son?" Could the suspicion he met in the hallways of the school, no matter how much he tried to reassure inquiring personnel, manifest as lowered expectations for his son's ability?

"It never seemed to occur to them that I was there out of genuine interest in the education of my son. I was greeted with distrustful facial expressions instead of a trusting smile." His emphasis on "genuine interest" reflects the depths of his dismay over how the school's staff could have mistaken his motives. "Why else would I be there?" he exclaimed.

Earl's personal identity as a father was challenged, forcing him into another clash with the ugly realities of stereotyping. The incident not only forced him to handle the negative impact upon himself, it muted what he wanted most to convey to his son—the image of a strong, caring, involved father. While he thought his presence at parent-teacher night dispelled one belief about absent fathers, he fell victim to another: be suspicious of black men.

Anger: Conspiring with Personal Demons

During another one of his therapy sessions, Earl expressed his fury over the way he has been treated by a psychologist at his son's school. Whenever Bobby got into trouble the school called his mother at work and never tried to reach Earl, assuming, he thought, that he was just another absentee black father.

When he and his wife attended a meeting at the school, the school psychologist—a white woman—directed her attention toward his wife, repeatedly soliciting her views and never once including Earl in the discussion or asking his opinion, even though he was sitting right next to her. When he got upset with her and said what *he* thought, the psychologist sat up straight, crossed her arms, and pulled back in her seat, agitated and a little frightened by the interruption. Earl surmised that this was her reaction to "intimidation" from "this tall, big black man." He was understandably distressed while expressing the desire that his views about his son be respected as much as those of his wife.

"What did she think I was going to do to her?" he said, letting his anger flow. His anger was focused on her presumptions about "that black male shit," as he characterized it, or what his maleness and sexuality meant to her.

Hiding in his indignation about his manhood not being respected were unexamined episodes from his past. Bobby's struggles in school reminded him of his own. He came to that meeting aware that schools have treated black boys badly, stifling their motivation and pride in learning, in spite of what is encouraged at home. He had to battle the rising fear of not being able to help his son, a feeling that angered him much more than the rejection by the school psychologist. His son's school experiences were also deeply troubling. He did not want Bobby's educational background to parallel his, resulting in academic failures or difficulties. Earl had dismissed academics early on, because he struggled with reading and nobody helped him—in part because of attitudes about his size and color—and because he was too embarrassed and proud to ask for help.

"Furthermore," he said, "wouldn't asking my white teachers for help just prove to white folks how dumb we are?"

This is another example of how the invisibility virus feeds on confusion.

The Invisibility of Black Male Fatherhood

To be a father is to fulfill a set of specific personal beliefs that you have about the role. It is certainly more involved and complicated than the biological implications. As in the pursuit of any goals, we evaluate ourselves as much by what we consider essential to the effort of being a strong, caring father, as we do by the criteria that others attempt to impose upon us.

The difficulties we encounter as we attempt to reconcile varying conceptions of the "proper" father are in part due to the paucity of recognition given to those who struggle and succeed in being a good father. Frustrations in African American fatherhood, therefore, are directly related to the pathology of invisibility—absent fathers *and* unrecognized fathers.

There is no way for good role models to outweigh bad role models in the collective public dialogue about black men. It is difficult for "the good black father" to serve as a guide in fulfilling adult obligations when his image is competing with, or buried under, the "no-good" black father publicity. Some African American men feel that the judgment of us is so absolute in its harshness that being a good father is unattainable. Given those terms along with the other challenges in our lives, there are men who don't even bother to make an effort because they feel it will never make a difference. It seems that we have forever been portrayed as absent, or at best indifferent to the responsibilities of fatherhood. Nevertheless, many African American men have been conscientious fathers. Perfect? no. Without faults? No. But fulfilling fatherly roles to the best of their abilities? *Yes!*

Fathers' Expectations—Guidelines for Educators

When we go to school to meet with our children's teachers, we do so intending to meet expectations as a good father and as a responsible man. Fulfillment of all or part of these expectations would reinforce our sense of fatherhood, marital partnership, and personal identity. In the visit to the school, we want affirmation as "the good black father." For example, Earl expected the school environment, school authorities, and schoolteachers to be hospitable and to welcome him as a concerned father, even *more* as a concerned black father. His reception should have come with an acknowledgment that gave him a sense of accomplishing his mission. He expected that discussions with the teachers, guidance counselors, and other school personnel would support his efforts toward the education of his son, and he hoped, on another level, that his presence—visibility—would be seen as supporting that interest.

When the experience turned sour, leaving in him the bitter taste of humiliation and being disregarded, his goals were compromised by his anger and indignation. The little acts of acceptance and regard that help verify one's sense of being the "good" father were nowhere to be found at the school. Resentment started to take hold as his attitude hardened toward the institution he entrusted with the education of his son. Earl detested the fact that the treatment he received from school employees put him in a defensive and retaliatory mood. He felt a surge of need to protect black male dignity and his own self-respect. At the same time, he knew that acting on the provocation he was experiencing could precipitate his coming across as intimidating and thus lead to repercussions his black son might feel as a result of the impression his father, the protector, left with his white teachers. It was a tightrope of misinterpretations that he walked every time he became assertive.

Little Slights Spill Over

As routine an event as visiting your child's school, like other daily encounters that are taken for granted by white parents, is complicated for black men. The thoughts and feelings African American men bring away from simple life situations that are perverted by racism often spill over to affect our behavior with others. Family, friends, and even coworkers may become unsuspecting outlets for the anger. Earl knew that when he got home he would have to discuss his visit to the school with his wife and son. Further complicating the episode was the fact that prior to his school visit he and his wife had a number of heated exchanges about the quality of his participation in Bobby's education.

The humiliation of the school incident merged with Earl's overall sense of how he and other black men can routinely be mistreated. Although he did not use the "usual" treatment of black men as an excuse, he did feel that this reality hampered his ability to personally change the quality of life for his family. Earl's impressions of his son's school environment were inextricably linked to deeply held passions about his own empowerment. In his inner thoughts and feelings he had to once again face and attempt to reconcile his own recollections of experiences as a student that carried obvious racial overtones. He had to evaluate just how successful he had been at handling those situations, as well as the effects they had on the course of his life. Once again he had to draw upon his spiritual strength so that he would not become captive to anger. He had to face making the hard distinction between what others did to him and what he did to himself.

But his most immediate concern was centered on his ability to discuss with his wife his perceptions of his personal treatment at the school, without becoming locked in another hot debate about his adequacy as a father. His wife's opinions of his effectiveness in handling a school visit were linked not only to their son's school performance, but to her confidence in Earl as a parental partner and husband.

Quiet As It Is Kept, We Want to Be Good Fathers

A graduate student I supervise works with groups of incarcerated African American adolescent fathers, all of whom profess they want to be good fathers to their children. Many make these comments because they don't have their own fathers around. This professing of a desire to be involved fathers is something I hear regularly from African American men. For the most part, however, they don't have a clue as to how or where to begin this commitment, beyond the fundamentals of the need to provide and protect. But there is willingness, desire, and passion, as well as frustration over the outcomes. Compared to the apparent certainty of African American women's child-rearing roles, there doesn't seem to be much clarity about what we as African American men should do as fathers in the child-rearing department.

Women seem to know how to expand their biological role into maternal roles so that the transition appears almost seamless. We have different views of our role as fathers than African American women have of their role as mothers. In our African ancestry, traditional rites of passage guided young men into manhood and clearly defined roles of fatherhood as well as those of husbands and leaders. The middle passage into slavery breached those clear definitions of gender responsibilities. Women, however, could more easily continue the maternal roles consistent with their legacy in ways that men were not permitted to. Fathering had to find new criteria.

When our African slave ancestors taught their young sons the ways of their manhood—African self-reliance through collective effort, defiance, pride—it put them and their sons at severe risk. Consequently, little has developed to replace manhood training, except that which has evolved from African American men surviving in a hostile land. Today, manhood training in the form of rites of passages programs for African American boys, and equivalent appropriate training for girls, is growing in popularity throughout the country. It is an illustration of the need and desire to put in place a formal, culturally relevant practice for raising our young sons to be responsible men in spite of barriers.

In my work and experience with African American men, I know that many love and care for their children—and they demonstrate it by putting their work first. Understanding just how precarious the role of provider can be, work is what we focus on most of all. So many of us fight for this right and are devastated when we cannot fulfill it according to our vision. Furthermore, we seem to get caught between competing expectations over what our work contributes to our families, communities, and society.

Joe's Dilemma

For Joe, our security guard, a major source of conflict with his wife was his frequent change of jobs. The "ghosts" of the mistreatment heaped on his father spurred his discontent on his jobs. His judgment was also impaired by fantasies about obtaining jobs he could not hold. Joe's difficulty in getting the "big-time job" was due in part to his reluctance to further his education and training. When his wife pointed out this inconsistency in his thinking he became defiant. When she said that he needed to do something to secure better income because of the children's needs he became outraged, feeling trapped and insecure.

Joe vociferously represented his changing of jobs to his children as a sign of his intolerance of racism, reinforcing his powerful father image, and underscoring what he thought was an important parental lesson. On the other hand, Joe's wife expected that as a father he would do whatever was necessary to help the family. If that meant dealing with racism on the job, then so be it. Others have done it before, she thought, why not he? Joe felt that she was asking him to compromise his values as a black man of not tolerating mistreatment on the job. This in turn fueled his feelings of being trapped. His wife felt he was using race as an excuse.

Bill's Dilemma

Bill, like Joe, was also concerned about control over external circumstances that gave him dignity and respect. It was important for him to be able to come home to his children as a successful father, not only as a provider but also as a role model of what education and hard work can accomplish. His wife felt he gave too much time to the job and not enough to the children. Bill's belief in "you have to work twice as hard in order to get half as much" drove his compulsion to stay on top of things at work. The restaurant incident where he encountered racial slights raised Bill's misgivings about his career success and its meaning. He struggled with an "impostor syndrome"—living in unfounded fear of being caught as a fraud, found out to be not as talented as his position and achievements suggested. The occasional encounters with racial slights made him self-conscious about being an African American male and ignited the fear that his *race* would be his downfall—a very shameful feeling Bill passionately wants to expurgate from his soul.

Doing It By Ourselves: The Curse of Feeling "Terminally Unique"

My wife says I am notorious for not admitting I'm lost, while I feel confident I will find my way. We African American men are equally notorious for holding within ourselves negative racial experiences, believing we will find our way out of the emotional maze. However, if we could learn to just share with each other we could help one another to find our way when lost in the challenges of being a man. One fault we have as men and fathers is that we often undertake the role and confront the responsibilities as if we were the first to venture down the path. We believe our life experiences are "terminally unique." We must prove to ourselves, to our families, and to others that we can continue the legacy of black male survival—often from the mistaken perspective of being unaided. Our dependence on our own resourcefulness and improvisation— the same attributes that have served African American men so well for generations—leads us to believe it will serve us well too. We silently draw upon our confidence and our arrogance that we will not become that unusual statistic—a "black man who failed to survive."

In my support groups for black men we talk often about the misguided notion of being "terminally unique." We explore how this belief prevents us from using each other as a resource, and exposes our distrust of each other and our inordinate self-reliance. It makes life's journey a lonely one, even when in a crowd of friends and relatives. And we begin to believe that this is what we are destined to experience as African American men.

In his book *Fatheralong,* John Edgar Wideman captures this sentiment as he displays the difference between his father and mother in their views of the world.

> The first rule of my father's world is that you stand alone. Alone, alone, alone. A fact about which we have no choice or say, carved in stone above the portal we enter when we arrive on this earth. Your work in the world is to grasp this truth, never lose sight of it, turn it so it catches light from all angles, squeeze it till its hardness, its intractability is alchemied into a source of strength. Accept the bottom line, icy clarity of the one thing you can rely on: nothing. My mother's first rule was love. She refused to believe she was alone. Be not dismayed, whate'er betides, God will take care of you. The nothing my father acknowledged was for her just as cold and hard and unbearable a truth, but it could not encroach beyond a circle she drew in the air around herself. Her God's arms were that circle and he was also inside with her.

Our awareness of what is at stake in the business of survival has forced many of us to create ingenious ways to protect and preserve the linkages between our dignity at home, our dignity at work, and our dignity in the community and in all other places where it matters to us.

Distancing Ourselves from Our Sons and Daughters

It is a challenge for African American fathers to teach their children about trust, power, control, respect, and dignity in relationships. As we struggle with frustrations imposed by attitudes toward us, along with our own insecurities, arrogance, and self-assuredness, our children look to us for guidance on how an African American man is empowered. If their impression is an extension of our frustrations, embitteredness, and impotency, then father-son, father-daughter relations will become tense reflections of our own confusion and disillusionment. Our internalized struggle with an invisibility virus will be seeded in our children (and future generations) by our relationship with them. Thus, we often create ways of behaving and being that embody how we feel we are *supposed* to be empowered.

Consequently, African American fathers often seek, in their own way, to communicate to their children that they are (sometimes by any means necessary) competent, self-assured persons in spite of how black men are represented. We consciously work to counter any misrepresentation of how we are. It is a must, if for no other reason than to preserve our dignity and self-respect. Unfortunately, the psychological distance of some African American fathers—uncommunicative, enigmatic, and intimidating—is the way some of us choose to create the precious aura of powerfulness for our children.

The mundane daily caretaking of children is not directly related to many men's conception of being a strong provider and protector. We all seek a special way of expressing our strength in fatherhood. If we fail to convey this special persona adequately, we feel not only that we will begin to lose our children's respect, but that we will establish a future basis for personal struggles with them. However, to the contrary of our well-meaning intentions, our often enigmatic, distant fathering stance gives the impression that we don't embrace a definitive parental role that we are comfortable with, suggesting that our "work" is elsewhere. I see it as a symptom of the invisibility syndrome.

In the Eyes of Our Children

For many African American children and youth, their life conditions are a statement about who we are as fathers and men. "Why didn't you effectively mobilize to hold schools accountable?" we imagine them saying or thinking; or, "Why didn't you to find alternative ways to educate us? Why didn't you keep our neighborhoods safe? And why did you contribute to our lack of safety? If we can't depend on our parents to take care of us, then who do we look to?"

Each time we look into the eyes of our sons and daughters we must reflect on our personal efforts to enhance their quality of life. This legacy plays a major role in maintaining the bonds of respect and love between us. It is an essential ingredient in their manhood and woman-hood. There is no hiding from our children the disparity between our quality of life and that of others. Any disparity becomes unfinished business left for the next generation—tasks that make up the inter-minable struggle for black equality. It's understandable that there would be a proclivity for despair and hopelessness in our children, upon realizing they must pick up and continue the struggle at a point not much further along than where we began.

Many of our children today, particularly our sons, are unprepared, not only for leadership roles and the world of work, but also for a world still captive to racism. This is an unspoken burden we don't want to own up to as African American fathers, and it is one source of our chil-dren's disregard and disrespect for us as parents and adults. It is almost as if they are saying, "You betrayed my future, so you have no right to place expectations and demands upon me in the present."

"Father Stories"

As I write these words I wait for the birth of my first grandchild—a child who will be born by the time this book is published. This will be a child who, at the moment of birth, takes his or her first step on the journey that many persons of African descent have gone on for gener-ations. For me, it is like another chance—a chance, perhaps, to do what upon reflection I feel I have not done adequately, or to repeat what I *have* done well as a parent. That means this grandchild will hear family stories. My penchant for storytelling as a tool for rearing children is cast in the tradition of my father, his brothers and sisters, my grandfa-ther, and the classic Southern storytellers I grew up around.

Taking my own advice a few years ago, I started interviewing African American elders in Mississippi. At the end of each interview I asked the men what singular words of wisdom they would want to convey to the next generation of young African American men on how to survive. One respondent, a lifelong mill worker who, along with his wife, had raised eleven children—all of whom graduated from college or professional schools—thought for a moment and said wistfully, "I would tell them to eliminate the word *can't* from their vocabulary."

Brothers love to talk and preach-cum-rap. We create our visibility by the powerfulness of the stories taken from the raw circumstances of our lives, no matter what the reality may be. The question becomes, will our stories, like Ralph Ellison's *Invisible Man,* show a discovery of self and contribute to constructive awareness? Will they show our genuine honor in the battle with injustice? Will our stories embolden our sons and daughters?

As noted by John Edgar Wideman in *Fatheralong:*

Father stories are about establishing origins and through them legitimizing claims of ownership, of occupancy and identity. They connect what's momentary and passing to what surpasses, materiality to ideal . . . they are about blood and roots and earth, how they must be repeated each generation or they are lost forever. If the stories dim or disappear altogether, a people's greatness diminishes, each of us becomes a solitary actor. The fighter fights alone, for riches or survival, or finds himself a puffed-up brawler, a sideshow performer of other people's stories about themselves, if there is no chorus remembering, connecting him to Great Time.

PART THREE

LOOKING BENEATH THE SURFACE OF OUR RELATIONSHIPS

"Brotherman!" is a special greeting among black men . . . it proclaims: Our bloodlines and soulforce are the same and we have a common fate—what happens to one happens to all.

—Herb Boyd and Robert L. Allen, *Brotherman*

The frontier of rage that exists
between black men and women
is an open wound slowly
dripping through the years,
causing us to miss each other, dismembered
by our needs and self-righteous vindication
of our egos . . .

—Askia M. Toure, "The Frontier of Rage"

7

FRIENDSHIPS AMONG BLACK MEN

Stan and Rich—"Can I Trust You to Help Me Be Somebody?"

When Stan returned to his office after an offending encounter, he looked for Rich, his fellow African American. However, he knew that he could trust the sympathy of his colleague only to the extent that there was no need for Rich to act with him in a public declaration of anger. Rich could only commiserate.

When faced with racial insults in the office, Rich was the voice of calm. His behavior grew out of his fear of the consequences of speaking up. He saw doing so as risking many of the gains he had made in his life. For his personal comfort, Rich chose peace and tranquility about racial matters, even if it meant tolerating a little racism. This attitude frustrated Stan, and he never stopped pushing for his office brother to "come out of the closet with his rage."

It would have been easy for Stan to reject Rich outright, because he considered him weak in his stand against racial prejudice, to swagger before him, bragging about how coolly *he* handles "mighty whitey." But in doing so he would not have become close enough to Rich to learn of his incisive thinking when it comes to racism. He would not have learned of Rich's wisdom about counterproductive behavior and his wise suggestions about positive alternatives.

The frequency with which racism had undermined Stan's achievements had left him with a great deal of skepticism, a fear that he might not be able to hold onto his accomplishments. This resulted in a desire to have his efforts legitimized right away, before they could be taken away. Ever contending with a jaundiced belief that something or someone would inevitably come along to pull the rug out from under his feet, Stan was perennially looking over his shoulder. His friend, then, served as buffer against the assaults on his worth.

Charlie—Seeking Validation

Charlie had worked in the textile plant for ten years doing a variety of increasingly skilled jobs. Both his immediate supervisor and the manager of the division had been supportive ever since the three of them started to work for the company. Back then the company was smaller. With two other coworkers they formed a little inner circle within the plant. After work they often went for drinks at the local bar. Their coworkers saw them as a tight-knit group of close friends. Eventually a white man was promoted to supervisor, despite having less experience and recognition for competence than Charlie had. Charlie was devastated. He could only conclude that his race was the reason for not getting the promotion, so he quit his job in angry protest.

A year later Charlie was still unemployed. His decision was causing problems in his marriage and his relationship with his children and his friends. Charlie could not resolve his smoldering suspicion and anger over what happened, and it continued to emerge with each new job interview. He was now on the warpath against the slightest racial indignity that he detected, and he enlisted his friends to side with his perceptions and feelings. If they did not, he challenged their blackness. If they persisted in not seeing his side of things, he shunned them.

We expect our male friends to share our approach to life, particularly in facing those challenges unique to being a man of African descent.

Charlie wanted his buddies to help him fight invisibility by supporting the way he liked to be, in spite of pressures by others to be otherwise. We expect our friends to help us stake out the psychological turf that represents our identity. They are expected to help us protect it, given our mutual views on how to be a black man.

Reciprocity is essential in friendships. It connotes a mutuality of interests and needs, plus it gives purpose to the way we complement each other's fulfillment of that friendship. It is likely that the issues we are struggling with are similar to those of our friends. All black men, in their own way, are contending with the issues presented by being black and male in America, even if they deny their importance. Each man, however, finds his own outlet.

There are some black men who are immersed in black male networks and others who are not. There are those who have many black male friends, others who have few, and those, like John, who have none. John walked into my office and was surprised to discover I was a black psychologist. He thought there were none, and I could see that he was annoyed that his human resources officer referred him to me, assuming that he would prefer a black psychologist. I was on the company's list of outside referral sources and I was often recruited by the human resources office, because many of their black employees requested a psychologist of African descent, feeling that we would understand their life circumstances better. John made it clear early in our discussion that he had few black friends and that he did not associate with black coworkers at the job because he felt it hurt his chances of getting ahead at work and in life in general. John did not return after our first meeting, and I subsequently had to educate his human resources office that there are black men who do not always want the services of—or, for that matter, to associate with—other men of African descent.

John's chosen identity and manner of behaving in the world set up negative assumptions and expectations about encounters he might have with other black men.

On Being a Partner, a Main Man

I have three buddies from childhood and we have been together for well over forty years. We have fought together as a unit and we have fought each other. We have struggled through our love lives, marriages, education, and finances. We have shared advice on raising our children and directing our careers as we deflected racism. We all eventually got our doctorates, and we now work to improve the education and future of our youth, families, and community. We are children of the 1960s civil rights era and we still subscribe to those values of freedom, liberation, human rights and equality so passionately embraced during those times. To some we are an anomaly, to some we are role models.

Among African American men best friends are called by many endearing labels. But their fundamental role remains the same: be a close, trusted companion in good and bad moments, over a long time. The kind of friend that says, "You call, I come." Our best friends have been colorfully and affectionately called "partner," "main man," "running buddy," "ace," "bosom buddy," and more. These distinctions of course set apart those to whom we have the greatest personal attachment. Best friends are important for special levels of trust, confidentiality, and support. Other friends may be extended this privilege occasionally, but not as exclusively as is our "main partner."

Black men can depend on their partners to affirm their view of the world and their status in it—their personal power.

When Joe enters his favorite neighborhood watering hole he looks for Sekou and Jamal. Nearly inseparable, they are known as the "holy trinity." They share a similar philosophy about life. They have been coming to this cocktail lounge for years, where, as the regular patrons say, "they hold court." Here the men are able to comfortably pontificate about life. Within this union they have found mutuality and a shared respect that they get nowhere else—neither on the job, nor, to a certain extent, at home. At home they must contend with different views of how they are doing as providers. For Joe, Sekou, and Jamal, this translates into how they as black men are overcoming the barriers they talk so much about. Their friendship helps lighten this burden and helps put expectations and success into perspective.

Friendship Networks

In *Slim's Table,* Mitchell Duneier chronicled simple but complex friendships among a group of black men who are daily patrons at Valois, a Greek-owned cafeteria on Chicago's South Side. At his designated table, Slim presides like a patriarch, dispensing wisdom and compassion over the trials and tribulations of other patrons. He has a special connection to the "regulars" and plays a meaningful role in their lives, which gives distinction to his own life and theirs. These types of meaningful networks of African American male friendship exist all over.

For example, my cousin, an elder of the family who's in his eighties, once took me on a visit to his daily hangout. This day was reminiscent of my childhood, tagging along after him on his daily routines. It was a balmy Mississippi afternoon and all the congregants were present at their usual daily forum in the garage. They had been doing this for years. Cars kept coming around from all over town to get expert repairs on their tires. But it was evident by the way drivers solicited the opinions of the men in the garage that they also were there to hear the wisdom of five elderly black friends. As I sat on a seat that had been removed from a car, I listened to Rev. T. dispense opinions to his group of friends perched on various makeshift seats in his tire repair shop, and I couldn't help but observe the respect and depth of their friendship.

Elliot Liebow's classic, *Talley's Corner,* is another major sociological look at the daily transactions of black men on the street in their local neighborhood. Likened to the gatherings of our ancient ancestors in African marketplaces, street corners provide outlets for a personal closeness among African American men. They represent a precious form of legitimization.

The three men on the corner in Spike Lee's film *Do the Right Thing,* a sort of Greek chorus, also symbolized deep bonding.

Much of what black male friends talk about when they gather is their view of the world, how they cope with it, and what they would do to change it. There is much giving of opinion. Key to our talks with one another is reasserting our confidence and offering one another reassurances about our capacity to survive—themes that are rife in our advice and in our storytelling. In essence, it is commentary on managing our manhood, when so much is designed to keep us invisible.

History's Shaping of Our Friendships

Models of friendship among African American men evolved from the rituals of African manhood and friendship to the tenuous relationships formed by culturally diverse African slaves who were strangers to one another. Customs and practices that clearly delineated cultural rules of trust, power, and control between African men and women were abrogated and corrupted by bondage. Slaveholders knew this. They contained and repressed any social behavior that reflected this inclination. These were the overt days of the repression of any distinct identity among African men that made them conscious of anything besides servitude. The legacy of betrayal and the guarded trust between African Americans, which was engendered during slavery, and in our subsequent efforts toward freedom, created a psychological atmosphere that influenced the growth of the black male psyche.

We were property, not humans, and therefore an economic and legal system was created to treat us this way. History documents the social climate and policies of these times and how it dictated a course of living for us. Consequently, the human experience of escaping from slavery and the perpetual striving to gain civil rights in this country has often pitted us against each other in debates about our full inclusion and the political and economic consequences of demanding it. National interests were often the first consideration deciding our inclusion, not a moral imperative. Subsequently, for the benefit of their personal comfort, the privileged followed the path of gradualism in granting us full inclusion. This so-called social progress has fueled strategy debates for attaining civil rights, amply illustrated historically in the philosophical differences between Frederick Douglass and Martin Delany, Booker T. Washington and W. E. B. DuBois, Dr. Martin Luther King Jr., Malcolm X, and Kwame Toure (Stokeley Carmichael). Their differences were over the best means for achieving inclusion. What manifested as passionate differences between these leaders of movements also exists in day-to-day relationships between African American men, each striving in his own way to be recognized and feel included in a society resistant to his presence.

Our political views around this theme get shaped and are tested within our friendship networks. We grapple with how to assert our rights and gain our privileges. What is inclusion anyway, given that tokenism only allows a few to rise and gain privileges? And what about the status and condition of the majority of men of African descent? Do we make them visible while we climb the ladder, or do we forfeit our heritage for a privileged status that whispers to us *don't look or give back?* And where does that place us in respect to our friends who seek those same goals? This is why there is so much suspicion of ways of facing bigotry that are different from our own. It becomes a means for assessing genuineness in our friendships and mutuality in our privileges.

Seeking legitimacy, what happens to your identity when your friends insist that to be black is to be a victim of racism? There is the sense of always being under siege. Your African and enslaved ancestry adds to your psychological stress. Your alertness to racial mistreatment becomes preoccupying, giving racism a stranglehold on your capacity to think and act independently. Victim mentality impedes your ability to take steps to improve, because, as the perpetual victim, you see "Mr. Charlie" as an impenetrable fortress blocking your way. Friends must see it this way, or they must assemble around a different network of friends where they can achieve philosophical consensus.

Racism is designed to keep you off balance. The cliché "Once you've learned the game, they change the rules" is rampant in our belief about American racism. However, sometimes we become so absorbed by the unfairness attendant to white supremacy and its well-nurtured, exclusive entitlements, that we lose sight of our ability to set our own agenda and to determine our own destiny. We find ourselves making the inferior superior, and the superior inferior, such as when bad is good and good is bad—or, as in the shifting school attitude of our young brothers, to be smart is dumb. Upon this cratered rock we build values and friendships. If we think about what we have created, it is debilitating—winding its way through every aspect of our lives, just like a virus slowly winding its way through our body.

Contending with white privilege does not mean disregarding your strengths, those things you can do for yourself. Losing sight of that is another manifestation of the invisibility virus. Among friends we can talk endlessly and eloquently about what is being done to us, but not about what we are doing to ourselves. Among our friends, we too often lose sight of our capacity to do for ourselves, to determine who we are and what we can be. This eroding of perspective on one's self makes us vulnerable to what others impose as identity upon us. That identity is too often victim. As though being floored by the flu, we speak from a prone position, while our true potential atrophies.

Alert for Betrayals

Obsequious "Uncle Tom" behavior, or manifestations thereof, is a contemptible coping style among us. On the other hand, as I've shown, we may revere the rebellious, uncompromising attitude, but must be leery of its consequences. So for many African American men a model of survival more likely lies somewhere in between these two extremes, depending upon the circumstances. We can acquiesce or protest as our judgment dictates. But our behavior is examined by our friends for what we are about over time—what we practice versus what we preach. Our friends look at how we hold each other accountable, our relationships with women, how we protect our dignity—in other words, whether we represent more talk than walk, or vice versa. These are criteria for membership in the brotherhood.

Brothers suspected of aligning with those who would oppress us are shunned. Distrust born of past experience lingers like an unholy spectre among African American men. Are you willing to trade your identity as a brother for opportunities that distance you from your friends? We demand to know. Remaining alert to this possibility is part of our individual sixth sense. Thus, betrayal is a haunting nemesis to our friendships. The bar is high for the proving of trust between black men, because underlying some of our interactions is an unconscious evaluation of what the other has, what it represents for our friendship, and how it symbolizes being a member of the brotherhood.

In the minds of many black men, the more we are different from what defines white males the better. The task of trying to handle the reality of an inescapable white world that relentlessly affects our lives and represses us drives some of us to avoid the stress and confusion of bicultural experiences. We immerse ourselves in either a predominantly black world or a predominantly white one. There are many of us who are comfortable with the psychological cloak provided by total immersion in an African American community.

Immersion into either world, or somewhere in between, has its own consequences. If one chooses to become more like what white men are, one has to shed those attributes that black men hold dear. This choice to fit in comfortably with white men is made at the risk of being ostracized by black men. To become more visible with an ensemble of mannerisms and thinking patterns consistent with white male acceptance is, in fact, rendering one's black identity invisible. Such an election of this personal identity for a black man alienates him from his black brethren and on some level makes him suspect by white men. Our friendships with each other either have to tolerate our switching back and forth, depending upon which company we are keeping, or will force us to choose for the sake of the comfort of our personal relationships. This puts a strain on friendships and a strain on trust. As a "down brother," your opportunities will not change you, nor how you relate to us, your friends.

Looking Good for My Friends

"Saving face" and "putting on a good face" are two important ego defense techniques used in protecting respect, dignity, and honor among us. Each man has his own particular way of putting on appearances or rectifying bad situations so that he does not look bad. Saving face is one of the most important aspects of maintaining self-respect. To many men, it is an essential part of being a man. Consequently, if manhood is associated with being strong, an able provider, a capable protector of loved ones, any incapacity in fulfilling those roles reveals weakness and vulnerability and is not for public view. This cannot be disclosed to friends—in some instances, not even to your main man, for fear of what he might say, or of what such disclosure will do to the relationship.

Earl's display of indignation over the disregard he experienced from the white school psychologist (a woman, at that) conveyed to me—another black man—that he protected his dignity. I was an outlet for his anger, given his presumption that I shared his anger. In the eyes of other black men, it is a shameful thing for a person like Earl not to have a means of saving face. On the other hand, invoking a racism victim defense is the easiest way to solicit empathy from our partners and to decrease the possibility of disgrace.

Saving face is also manifested in confrontations that evolve between gangs. A group of young brothers are walking down the street and someone doesn't like the manner of eye contact in the other, so angry words are exchanged, a fight occurs, and gunshots follow. Within our friendship and acquaintance circles, black men kill and maim black men in far greater numbers than any other group has (Ku Klux Klan, skinheads, police, and enemies in war)—all over violations of respect and saving face.

Trust in Black Male Friendships

Carlos knew, when he entered the next room where his friends were, that he had to walk a certain way and greet them in the usual manner of speaking and embrace. He thought about how automatic it was. His behavior, that they all trusted each other to display faithfully, was like a badge for entry into this circle of close friends. It reaffirmed membership in the brotherhood, a necessary precursor for building other areas of their friendship. Carlos knew there was a checklist of behaviors, beliefs, and attitudes that his friends relied on his having to elevate their friendship to genuine closeness. They must have confidence in reasonably knowing what Carlos and any other member of the group is going to do. Carlos' friends knew, for example, how he felt about his job, women, and barriers to getting ahead in life. They expected him to remain consistent in his beliefs and would tease him, challenging him with exceptions to his views to test how strongly he held onto them. Carlos knew too much deviation in his behavior would bring instant suspicion from the group and potential ostracizing. He had heard, "Where're you coming from, man?" thrown in the face of too many guys to not monitor what he said and did when among the brothers.

Power in Action in Our Friendships

Earl's humiliation by the white female school psychologist extended beyond his wife's feelings about the incident to include the fact that his close friends chided him about the way he handled it. They felt he should have done more than just become indignant. They thought he should have followed it up by filing a formal grievance with the principal. "Schools have to learn that there are concerned black fathers out there—and men who need to be treated with respect," Earl said, agreeing with his friends. Much to the chagrin of his wife, Earl filed a grievance, talked to the principal, and proposed a fathers' meeting with school authorities to redress the stereotypical notions of fathers' roles at the school, particularly black fathers. His partners were impressed.

Control as a Factor in Friendships

Whenever we feel there is a violation of our dignity, we must rectify the humiliation. It is particularly important that our partners are able to witness this ability from time to time.

Sonny was chatting in the corner at a party with his friends when suddenly he jumped up, dashed across the room and grabbed his wife, Cathy, by the arm and escorted her out of the room. His partners laughed and gave each other fives, for they had been teasing him about another brother's alleged interest in his wife, thus fueling Sonny's infamous jealous streak. At the urging of others, Eli went after his friend to make certain Sonny didn't do anything stupid, such as abuse Cathy or try to confront the brother who he believed was making a move. They all joked and approvingly acknowledged Sonny's actions by citing the closely held value among brothers: don't mess with a brother's woman, money, or food.

How Success Splits Friends

The "brotherhood" among African American males can be very strong and demanding regarding the expectation to stand together—both literally and figuratively—against the "man." "Us-against-the-man" expectations, or suspicions about white male intent, vary among groups of black males. It ranges from the (atti)"tude" typical of young men, to political coalitions among various black business and professional groups. "Not selling out" (to the interests of white people) is important and remains a significant expectation among black men. Opportunities for upward mobility that can move us away from our circle of friends can have a crushing impact on our ability to accept success.

The interesting bind presented by black men's success is that it is both desired and damned at the same time. What it does to our friendships is reflective of this dilemma. A "brother's" success implies independence, power, and control over his life. Success means you have removed the symbolic shackles of African American male oppression. This could be evidenced by owning material goods such as better clothes, a fine car, a beautiful house, and other indicators of your rise in status.

A liability attached to success in our community is the tension, jealousy, and envy it creates. Living your success leaves you open to criticism of being too good to associate with average black people. Therefore, one of the ways we respond to the affluence of others is to demean and undermine its importance, even while striving for the exact same status symbols. It is one of the greatest threats to our friendships. What will our partners think about our success? On the one hand we will rightfully expect a successful person's commitment to and reinvestment in the community, but we will discredit the efforts and means that make the reinvestment possible. That's crazy!

Members of the black middle class are routinely put to this litmus test and scrutinized for the possibility of being "sellouts," although scores of its members have given leadership and other valuable resources to the community for generations. The efforts of the black middle class to become educated, to network, to sacrifice, and to work within the system—or independent of it—often breeds suspicion among those of us with less, or who are under extreme duress from discrimination and prejudice. We start putting demands upon successful brothers sometimes unrealistically.

This unfortunate attitude begets behavior that mimics "crabs in the barrel"—as one reaches the top, another crab below it, grabbing for higher levels, pulls it down. At times, this pulling down from below is a deliberate process of leveling and humbling the individual to ensure that "his head does not get too big." Friends and relatives have a way of doing that. It may also be an unconscious action to limit the progress of a successful friend, because that success only reminds us of our own failures, lost opportunities, and social abandonment. This type of behavior fulfills the adage, "divided we fall." Others more powerful and with their own agenda can bring down a divided house. If we are uncertain how gaining privileges defines our identity as well as opportunity, as men of African descent, we risk losing our heritage. Our challenge is to show its value to our success. Such a decision makes our heritage visible in ways society has not before chosen to see.

Bad-mouthing one another's success only attacks our friends' personal creation of visibility, or their means of becoming somebody—an important aspiration. It should not be necessary to disrespect a vital structure of achievement through which the friend has overcome racism, prejudice, and discrimination. Moreover, this propensity to act like "crabs in the barrel" has been exploited by racists for generations.

Getting Rid of "Putting Down" and Boasting over Small Gains

In our friendships we must be alert to our own behavior—both verbal and nonverbal—where it detracts from the legitimate accomplishments of a friend. If there is envy welling from within, we must introspectively seek its source. We must be honest in seeing it for what it is. We must ask if we truly know what our own talents and abilities are. Have we stuck with whatever it takes to develop them? Have the friends we have envied done what we have failed to do, such as create the independent means and will for developing talents sufficiently? We must learn to accept and acknowledge our God-given talents, but we must also do something constructively with them.

The comedienne Jackie "Moms" Mabley once said, "If you always do what you always did you will always get what you always got."

It is left to each man to make an honest commitment to self-development and to exercise the required self-discipline to nurture his talents. "You reap what you sow," as we so often hear our elders say. And not everyone sows with the same quality seeds. We each have unique contributions to make and must harvest them appropriately.

Unwarranted boasting or bragging over small gains in our friendship circles is often a cover-up for our own uncertainty and confusion. The "I'm bad" bravado gives the impression that we are in control, that we are powerful.

To reduce the games of intimidation black men play with each other requires identifying what angers us, and how to gain resolution for our indignation. All too often we let tangible things, like the gun in our hand, substitute for resolution when our instincts tell us more is required, such as negotiations.

Friendship between black men must be more than colluding to protect each other's image. Our aggressive, "put-down" behavior toward each other is really acting out the need for recognition, satisfaction, legitimacy, and validation. Our current patterns of friendship are adequate within a framework for survival, but they are insufficient within a framework of family and community empowerment.

I encourage men to cultivate the goal of positive personal development and fruitful collaboration by asking the following questions:

- Do behavior and attitudes within your network of friends work to eradicate or perpetuate the stereotypes and attitudes that oppress us?
- What is it that your partners do for you? To what degree do they contribute positively to your growth?
- Do your personal friendships within the brotherhood help the African American family and community? If so, in what ways, and if not, why not?

8

RELATIONSHIPS WITH BLACK WOMEN

Can We Talk?

"I cannot tell you how many times I have been in conversations about relationships between black men and black women," Charles said as he sat in my office openly displaying his frustration. At age thirty-one, Charles had been recently laid off from his job as a bank teller. "Every party or nightclub I go to I get into one of those conversations. Now I'll have to explain why I have no job. No matter what you say, you're damned if you do or you're damned if you don't. It's a no-win situation, but it's hard to avoid those conversations," he explained.

One day as I was riding on the A train a group of young black men boarded. They were talking loudly and everyone in our section of the subway car could hear them. One of the boys they called Jermott proclaimed, "Man-n-n, don't let that bitch jerk you around. They always trying to play with your mind." His friends' laughter reverberated around the car, signaling their agreement.

Meanwhile, black women keep looking for ways to get meaningful relationships with black men. Charise, a single mom of a six-year-old boy, was a student in my class called "Relationships: Black Men and Black Women." One day, as we were leaving the class, she asked, "What's up with black men? Do they have some kind of commitment phobia?"

Charles, Jermott, and Charise reflect the pain, hope, and—yes—love entwined in the relationships between black men and black women. While heated conversations on the topic can be launched instantly, it is difficult for black men to have serious discussions with black women. This is no less true for women, although they will justifiably claim to be more open to such discussions than are men.

On one occasion, my wife and I were attending a party where the women were sitting outside on the deck laughing and talking as many of the men were downstairs watching a football game on TV. The women were discussing the movie *How Stella Got Her Groove Back.* Set in the tropics, the movie's plot involves a romance between an older black woman and a younger black man. My wife and her friends invited the guys to join the discussion. Many of the men saw the invitation as a dare and warned the rest of us to stay away. The scene was too reminiscent of similar discussions about the Clarence Thomas–Anita Hill controversy, or Terry McMillan's earlier successful book and movie, *Waiting to Exhale.*

What is it about the topic of black men–black women relationships that raises so many anxious emotions, opinions, and attitudes? Why is it that when men discuss it, black women are at the center of the conversation, and when women discuss it, black men are at the center of the conversation? Why is it that neither women nor men can make our partnerships central to the conversation without the apprehension that there will be revelations of disappointments? Troy and Susan's story offers some insight.

Struggling for Control: Susan and Troy's Story

Troy and Susan came to me because of a growing strain in their marriage. They knew their marriage would fail if they did not do something about their problems. Troy did not have much faith in counseling, but Susan warned that he would be to blame if their marriage failed because of his lack of cooperation. Troy did not want her to be able to claim that, so he grudgingly attended the counseling sessions. The couple said their attempts to communicate frequently ended in heated arguments. Troy responded to the arguments by lapsing into defiant episodes of silence, refusing to be engaged, and often leaving the home. He accused Susan of being a nag who worried about everything, driving Troy and the children crazy with what he considered her "executive orders" and her endless dissatisfaction with him.

Susan was particularly upset over his lack of attention, their waning sex life, and his questionable career motivation. She accused Troy of having an affair. He denied the accusation and cited her constant need to blame him. He felt that the decline in their relationship and sexual intimacy grew out of Susan's preoccupation with the children, her job, and always trying to be, as he noted sarcastically, "boss of the household." Susan felt that his aloofness to family affairs meant that he had no interest in them. The romance they enjoyed during their courtship had been overwhelmed by the concerns of raising children and making money to purchase a house.

These are common marital complaints I encounter in counseling couples. However, for a young couple, being of African descent presents special challenges. Troy and Susan wanted to raise respectful, good children. From their own childhood experiences they knew they had to guard against their children attending inferior schools or being placed in classrooms where the teachers have low expectations of their performance. As a result, they both pushed the family to achieve.

In fulfilling his vision as provider, Troy saw the inequities in assignments and in promotions on his job as a threat to his role, but he felt that he was maneuvering his career forward in spite of those circumstances. But to stay alert and maintain the requisite vigilance created an additional stress. He was hard on himself, frequently reassessing his judgment and seeking advice from coworkers and friends that he trusted. This was an effort that further taxed his views of trust, power, and control, especially when he took into account previous bad direction and betrayals by people, policies, and practices on the job. The job made nothing of his concerns, only caring about the comfort of his coworkers and how his presence affected the work atmosphere.

He tried not to take it home to Susan and the kids, but sometimes he failed, becoming pensive, disengaged, and irritable—always attempting to think through his next move in the never-ending chess game of overcoming attitude barriers at work. It was difficult to not use this mind-set as a rationale for their marital struggles.

Troy felt Susan did not support him enough. When he came home and discussed his job, he felt that her response was to launch an "inquisition," scrutinizing his judgment and dismissing his views as whining. Susan felt Troy thought too much about things and took too long to act. "I'm a doer, he's a thinker," she often remarked. "All you're trying to do is hold me by my balls," Troy fired back one time with angry indignation, provoking an argument right in the midst of our counseling session.

Troy's pride did not allow him to tolerate humiliation. Victory is so much a part of being a man in the brotherhood that defeat is absolutely unacceptable. When others have more of a say in what we do and how we should live than we do, our instinct is to resist.

The History Between Us

The personal and intimate relations between African American men and women dates back to Africa where there were clearly defined, traditional roles for men and women. These roles were obliterated by the cruel economics of slavery.

In slavery there was equality in the physical abuse and psychological havoc wreaked upon black men and women. Out of this cauldron new gender roles emerged. African men and women in captivity had to invent and then employ altogether new ways of relating to one another, and new strategies to protect each other, to survive the devastating humiliation and brutal physical assault delivered by the pernicious business of slavery.

Any question of male supremacy or dominating female matriarchy was lost in the struggle for survival. One can surmise that a special closeness and intimacy existed between black men and women during this time. Any individual could be sold away from his or her family, regardless of the commitment to each other. We can assume time together was highly valued. Each person had an urgent need for support from an intimate partner. Heroics in finding separated loved ones characterized this closeness between us.

Sankofa, the movie, and *Roots,* the televised miniseries, dramatically captured some of this closeness. There we saw vivid portrayals of the depth and complexity of interpersonal relationships between bondsmen and women. Examples are also preserved in the historical records of such couples as Lucy Terry Prince and Abijah Prince, Nancy and Gabriel Prosser, William and Ellen Craft, and Frederick and Anna Douglass.

The relationships built out of the miserable uncertainties of the "peculiar institution" changed again with emancipation. Then, black men and women were freed to establish more stable families and different roles. But with this freedom came the difficulties of providing sufficient income and resources. Freedom brought another form of bondage. This one was built on economic servitude and social stigma—a circumstance that was almost as impossible to control as were the exigencies of slavery.

Freedom brought expectations of inclusion in the American dream of the "ideal American family," with all the gender trappings of conventional European society. To retain vestiges of African family customs and traditions, we thought, would only reinforce notions of the uncivilized savage. Consequently, the route toward acceptance as African Americans was paved with presumptions of conformity to white standards. However, at the same time, the black community— which has remained socially segregated until this day—was systematically denied access to the economic and educational requirements to *achieve* the "American dream." It is within this context that the current psychological dynamic—the mating dance—between black men and women has evolved.

Women As Trophies

I have spent countless hours and days in various historically black colleges and universities as a student, a parent, a lecturer, a consultant, or a conference participant and visitor, so I recognize that it is customary for black male students to rate the beauty of the newly arrived freshmen women. In one particular instance, a group of males gathered outside the women's dormitory with a set of flash cards, numbered from one to ten. Like judges in competitive figure skating or swimming events, the young men would hold up a number as the women entered and exited the building. The higher the number the more favorable the rating. Needless to say, the raters' judgments were reinforced by a crowd of young men shouting out such exclamations as: "She's fine," "She's phat," or "A heartstopper" for the higher ratings, "A wannabee," or "Needs a little work" for the middle-range ratings, to "Ghost killer," or "Jungle bunny" for the lower ones.

I was as surprised by the public boldness of the episode as I was pained by the emotional abuse of the women and the persistence over generations of our tendency to label African American female beauty based on European standards. Women with lighter skin and with more Anglo features tended to get higher ratings. And there I stood at the close of the twentieth century watching this legacy cruelly acted out in a privileged generation that will live most of its lifetime in the twenty-first century.

Interestingly enough, tension and conflict are not necessarily the defining relationship most of us have with black women. On the contrary, many of us have a special intimate relationship with some black women to whom we disclose our true thoughts and feelings. There are in fact some black women with whom we are less guarded than we are with men. With these special sister-friends we are more willing to share our personal fears than with each other. So where does our callousness come from? What stands in the way of publicly respecting black women? Once again, the invisibility syndrome offers numerous clues.

Gaining Status Through the Woman on Your Arm

One of the ways African American men gain visibility is through their association with women whose appearances they believe will find approval within their critical networks (mainly among black male friends). And, on an unspoken level, if those looks meet criteria promoted by white society, so much the better. The choice of a partner, one of the few things black men have some control over, is vital to our status and self-esteem.

Being labeled a "ladies' man" or "womanizer," implies high status and expert skill. There is pride in the capacity to "get" a woman, especially if she is someone other black men consider good-looking and desirable. The reward of having the desirable woman who is prized by other black men is a cherished stamp of distinction in the brotherhood.

As I talked to Carl, Les, and T. R. in the hallway of their high school, the bell rang for a change of class. Their talk with me ended as the hallways filled with students and their eyes turned to follow "the young mommies" making their way to the next class. "Having a fine mama is important, Doc, it makes you somebody. Every brother is out to get one."

The worth of the reward for "winning over" a beautiful woman is determined by your group of friends, their identity, and their criteria for beauty. Depending upon the broad appeal of a woman's beauty, one's status can be elevated a notch above the members of one's friendship network. It is this emotional and psychological outlook that forms the assumptions tied to the numerous black male labels for black women, such as "the fox," "phat," "fine mama," and even the controversial and demeaning use of the label "bitch." When another black male refers to your girlfriend using one of the above labels, your status is immediately enhanced.

Therefore, for numerous black boys the initial lessons for becoming the "good black man" that come from other black men are heavily associated with one's talents to charm and win the woman prize.

Demonstrating an ability to rap and to get a girl is a first major test of manhood for teenage boys. We begin to cultivate these skills early, and we often find willing mentors in our fathers, older brothers, uncles, and friends. The dreadful downside of this mentoring transforms the black woman into a conquest rather than a partner.

"Who you have on your arm is symbolic of one's persuasive ability, attractiveness, and competence as a man," said Ed, a doctoral student in psychology who decided to do his dissertation on African American male and female relationships. I was intrigued by his use of the words "competence as a man." When I asked him what he meant and why he wanted to study this topic, he replied, "The stakes are so high for having the right sister that some brothers don't even enter this game. I'm interested in the brothers who are tired of playing the game."

As Ed notes, "playing the game," or having the right woman to gain approval from other African American men, from our mothers, fathers, important family members, or within the African American community, is essential for status and recognition. Our status is greatly enhanced when the woman in our lives demonstrates that we are good judges of feminine beauty. Interestingly enough, this implies that we are capable of using good judgment in other areas of our lives. The right woman on our arm can actually suggest that, when it comes to important decisions, we can be trusted to make good ones.

Through the woman he selects, the black man's presumed competence in this area is extended to other domains, such as giving others advice about women, strategic planning (sometimes known as scheming), handling other men, and dealing with family members.

Many men work as hard at getting "the good woman" as they do on their basketball, golf, or tennis game. It has become a sphere—designated by a wide consensus among African American men—where unique skills are required to obtain a clearly defined goal. The woman is the trophy and the measure of one's power.

And when men win the trophy the game is over. But for women the purpose of the relationship has just begun. For women the relationship is about playing the game of life. This conflict of purposes is one of the early sources of our difficulties in relationships.

Overcoming a Conflict of Purposes—Why Commitment Feels Like a Trap

For many African American men it is difficult to remain in the relationship once it is secured, because the conquest was very often the sole motivation. An enormous emphasis is placed on gaining skill in the "pursuit" and "conquest" of a woman. Among African American men there exists little or no conversation when we gather and talk on the purpose, role, and skills required of a proper partner in a relationship after it has been established. This is why commitment in our relationships often eludes us. This is why commitment feels like a trap. We enter relationships unprepared to make them successful. Unfortunately, in far too many instances we are uncertain of, or haven't given serious thought to, the long-term purpose of the relationship. And perhaps most important of all, we have not been trained to see how to derive recognition from success in relationships.

Although male–female partnership and family is a universally valued outcome for relationships, it is not necessarily a primary goal for black men, particularly for those unclear about its importance. Therefore, African American men must find a new purpose that is as motivating and meaningful for the success of a relationship as is the process of establishing it. I regularly say to men with whom I work, "After finding your honey, you must know how to work with your honey."

The twin pillars of beauty and sex comprise too much of the foundation on which we build our relationships with black women. The mating game is a "playing field" to which we feel we have complete access. Here, we are less encumbered by race than we are in other important arenas, such as the job market. In our relationships with black women we impose the dominance of our male, self-serving interests. Tragically, we frequently fail to move beyond sex and beauty in our relationships.

Underestimating What Women Know

African American men and women, like most couples, are individuals, each with beliefs about his or her capacity to achieve personal goals, including the capacity to be partners. How successful we have been in overcoming social factors that marginalize African American people is a paramount factor. How much are we aware of, and prepared to contend with, each other's issues as invisible persons in society? More importantly, how prepared are we to help ourselves and our partners in this struggle? I have found that few black men assume that women should be concerned about such questions.

John and Carol have been married for five years and have a one-year-old son. He is a third-generation African American with family roots in the south. Carol's family has been in New York City for three generations. John noted in a couple's session, "She's never fully understood what a black man has to go through in this country."

"What are you talking about?! I've seen what my brothers and uncles have gone through, and they've done all right. You're too scared to speak up for your rights," Carol retorted.

John gave me a furtive glance and fired back at Carol, "What do you mean? I'm taking care of you and my son, so why are you always complaining?"

"Because I know you can do better," said Carol, "and we're here so we can talk about it, without you always walking away from me angry."

Fear of Being "Read" by Our Partners

This type of observation and challenge from black women is not well-received by black men, despite how accurate it may well be. Often our initial feeling is that our judgment is disrespected and our way of doing things unappreciated. Our very dignity is threatened.

The point was not how valid Carol's observations may have been. John felt it was up to him to figure out how to assert and protect his rights. Admission to our partners of personal uncertainty or doubt is a very uncomfortable disclosure for most black men. For many it is considered downright unmanly. It particularly is forbidden if we are uncertain about how the disclosure will affect our partner's perception of us.

Viewing the woman as an adornment rather than as a partner has significant ramifications for how we view ourselves. A most common one is the attitude that the woman has no say in how we live our life as black men. This outlook is a direct outgrowth of a significant need for a sense of authority—a sense of authority that is out of reach in numerous areas of daily life. I have encountered many men in therapy—and otherwise—who manifest an underlying notion that partnership and compatibility with a black woman means that she will not unduly challenge his authority and self-esteem. As Joe once exclaimed, "I want no hassles from my woman."

In his book *Black Men: Obsolete, Single, Dangerous? The Afrikan American Family in Transition,* Haki Madhubuti notes that: "Most Black men fear analysis of their actions from anybody, especially the sisters with whom they are living or relating. This denial of reality is not uncommon among Black men. Obviously, the woman a brother is with knows him better than anyone, with the possible exception of his parents and siblings."

Too often, the less a black woman "reads her man" the more she is considered a "good black woman." A fear of being discovered as powerless and not in control of events within our own world makes us extremely sensitive to criticism from our mate, even when it's constructive. We do not want to face this unmasking of our image. It exposes—particularly to our intimate partner—the pain of helplessness that evolved from the legacy of moving from leg irons to unemployment lines.

Turning a Relationship into a Partnership

Overcoming our need to be right and our fears of being wrong is a first step in turning our relationships into partnerships. Each of us as African American men and women have faced our own challenges of surviving and protecting our sense of self, in spite of racism and other hurdles put in our paths by life—including those hurdles we ourselves created. Because of these personal experiences it is hard to be open to the critical analysis of the behavior of others. We both feel we have to be "right" in the positions we take with each other. We each tend to display a defensiveness nurtured by our highly developed intuitive sixth sense that warns us when we are staring pretense and deception in the face. As black folks, an enormous amount of our energy is spent learning to detect genuineness when we encounter members of other races. At the heart of this effort is a legacy of betrayal.

Thus, that legacy of betrayal strengthens its stranglehold on our ability to be good working partners. It results in our inability to trust the judgment of others (including our loved ones) because we have become so dependent on our own instincts for survival. We want to feel that we have influence over the course of our lives. A partnership should enhance that feeling, rather than threaten it. African American men and women must find complementary roles and tasks that allow each partner a sense of purpose and accomplishment. In other words, both parties in a relationship must find ways that our individual efforts achieve mutual goals.

Ken and Dorell—Trying to Make Ends Meet

Ken and Dorell had been arguing about her desire to quit her job as a nurse's aide and return to school to finish studies for her nursing degree. Ken wondered who would care for their two children, five and eight years old, given the demands of nursing school. Furthermore, he was very concerned about their finances. He wondered how they would make ends meet without Dorell's salary.

Ken had his own plans. He wanted to start a small business and was saving toward that goal. With Dorell returning to school, he saw his dreams of owning a business vanishing. Ken felt that, given a few years, he could get his business going and then become financially capable of allowing Dorell to return to school. But for Dorell, these were the same old promises that had delayed her return to school since the birth of their children. She also felt that her husband didn't support her. Ken believed that starting his own business would free him from what he called "the last hired, first fired syndrome." He had witnessed black men in his sales office being victimized by this syndrome more than any other group. On the other hand, Dorell was not as confident as Ken that he would be any freer of racism as an entrepreneur.

Ken and Dorell found it difficult to move beyond their individual interests, and their arguments ended in finger-pointing. During the counseling session they interrupted one another before their thoughts could be completed. This behavior served only to anger both of them. They were so locked in their individual positions that they were unable to see the big picture.

Upon close examination, one could see that Ken's rate of progress toward his new business would not be jeopardized by the time it would take Dorell to finish nursing school. Her graduation would actually help him fulfill his dream by providing the family with greater financial potential. By earning her nursing degree, Dorell would be helping the family by helping herself and Ken's business objectives.

The Arrogance of Ignorance

When you look at Ken and Dorell's marriage you see a typical marital power struggle. However, deeply embedded in these dynamics is the unspoken conundrum internalized by Ken, which is that if we cannot control and exude stature in our relationships with black women, and other black men for that matter, then how can we contend with white males? This is an example of how black masculinity gets caught up in the thinking of white male supremacy—power at the expense of people rather than power in partnership with people. Male domination in relationships is a conventional idea. We are expected to exhibit this as much in our ability to stand up to the system of white male racism as we are to stand up to challenges from black women. Given our marginality in society, "getting-over" behavior, or, in other words, masking our true motives, is a product of the invisibility syndrome. To brothers, and oddly as it may seem, even to some black women, this makes "a really good black man."

This twisted understanding of what makes up the "good black man" is thoroughly infused in black male and female relationships. A particular liability of this male domination posture, as well as "getting-over" behavior that exemplifies it, is the inability to admit a lack of understanding or not knowing, for fear of being found out. This is the arrogance of ignorance. As poet Haki Madhubuti candidly observes, "Until black men can honestly face themselves and communicate with themselves, they will not be able to relate meaningfully to Black Women. Understanding one's self starts with an admission of not understanding."

From Rapper to Provider: A Fallacy Haunts the Ladies' Man

The transition from competence as a rapper in our youth to that of provider in adulthood can present major problems for us. The very same forces that make the transition necessary in the first place conspire to thwart it. Unstable and insecure employment can make meeting the needs of a relationship virtually impossible. As a rapper attempts to become the provider he finds himself in the troublesome position of having a decreasing sense of mastery over his life. Upon becoming the provider, there opens a deep chasm between what's considered important or of value, and what's seen as the path to dignity and respect. For those of us who placed so much energy and worth on getting into relationships, the discrepancy in the provider role is painful: We were in greater control of our image as the "ladies' man."

The fallacy in the "ladies' man" theme is its singular focus on how to get with a woman, instead of how to partner with a woman to provide for a family. What do perfect charm, seducing, and "getting-over" behavior have to do with the essentials of genuine intimate partnerships or marriage? These "ladies' man" skills are almost entirely unrelated to the more serious obligations of manhood—provider, father, and community leader. Equally fallacious is the belief that this behavior suggests something about our capacity to nurture, once in a relationship.

However, our beguiling style—that some of us perfect to art form— can charm a woman into believing that the emotions attached to the seductive lover behavior will in fact extend into other nurturing roles required to sustain a relationship. But many of us do not connect our feelings and the behavior exhibited in seduction and sexual intimacy to emotional accessibility. That is, the expressive repertoire employed in wooing is very different from providing emotional, nurturing support to a mate overwhelmed and needy from the struggles of daily survival.

Moreover, the way that intimacy was experienced during courtship needs to be transformed in a committed relationship. Those men who successfully make the transition into becoming good providers, partners, and parents have found fulfillment for themselves and intimacy in these new roles. We have to find something in the circumstances of the relationship that gives us motivation to make the partnership work. We rarely talk about it. Whatever it is, it must be something we are willing to sacrifice for and work for; it must bring us self-respect, while at the same time allowing us to be alert to the circumstances faced by the larger brotherhood of African American men. This choice can be as diverse and idiosyncratic as there are men in the community.

Karl said to the members of a support group for black men, "I'm afraid to admit that I don't want to be with my five-year-old son, don't want to take the time. My father left me when I was young, so I feel guilty, and want to give him what I didn't have. But I am not sure I'm ready to devote the time and energy to be a father."

By contrast, Tom, a New York City transit worker, stood at my side while I snapped family pictures at a Howard University graduation. He reflected that "this is what it's all about, my twenty-five years down on those dangerous subway tracks, getting the first generation of this family through college."

Henry, perceived as a very quiet, unassuming man, watched while his wife and children flitted among the guests at their fiftieth wedding anniversary and responded to my question, "How did you stay married so long [as a black man, I thought]?"

"I did it all for that woman over there," he said, pointing across the room to his gray-haired wife. "I brought home my paycheck and she took care of me."

As these comments attest, Ken and Dorell have the means to flourish as supportive partners if they are willing to lay the groundwork. But several problems intervene.

The Problem of Competing Priorities

Commitment involves investing oneself in a relationship over an extended period of time. It consists of sharing resources, insights, support, and emotional intimacy. It includes sharing the joys and sorrows and the triumphs and disappointments that come with life. Commitment exists when an expanse of time shows that, by your words and deeds, you have been responsible and dependable and that you have been there for each other.

Remember Charles, eighty years old when I interviewed him in his living room in Mississippi? Charles said that he was able to persevere because "my wife and I had children to raise."

But it is more common for men to feel that their women hold them back or stand in their path. Unlike Charles, black men often believe they must go it alone. Women more often think of working together. Men regularly place the protection of their dignity first, while women place survival of their family first. Satisfaction in a relationship is much greater when partners share a common goal and commitment to how that satisfaction is achieved.

The noted African American sociologist Andrew Billingsley, in *Climbing Jacob's Ladder: The Enduring Legacy of African American Families,* concludes from findings of a national survey of black American families headed up by James Jackson at the Institute for Social Research at the University of Michigan, that six major functions of marriage were found as very important among the couples surveyed: child rearing, companionship, a sustained love and sex life, a sense of safety, help with housework, and financial security. African American men are scrutinized by black women for their capacity to meet all six of these expectations.

Those who do not "fit the bill" reduce the pool of eligible black men for women who hold these standards and embrace the values of families. Achieving a lasting relationship is so daunting for women it can transform the meaning of commitment. This reality forces some African American women to "settle," and to give up looking for men who meet their expectations.

The Scarcity of Viable Male Partners

In the justified opinion of many black women, the marginal position of Africans in America has created a scarcity of "good black men." The scarcity of such African American men does not go unnoticed by the men themselves. Unfortunately, it contributes to a cavalier attitude about commitment to relationships. It also fosters lascivious behavior. Robert Staples and Leanor Boulin Johnson share an extensive analysis of African American bachelorhood, partner selection, gender roles, and marital patterns in their book *Black Families at the Crossroads.* According to Staples and Johnson, the ratio of African American women to African American men is 100 to 85. This disparity in numbers is further enlarged by the fact that black women live longer than black men.

In many respects there is a statistical parallel to the psychological phenomenon of the invisibility of African American men. In their book *Looking at the Decline in Marriage Among African American Couples: Causes, Consequences, and Policy Implications,* M. Belinda Tucker and Claudia Mitchell-Kernan give compelling information that there are not only fewer African American men in absolute numbers, but when you consider other factors that influence standards for mate selection for African American women and men, the scarcity issue is greatly multiplied. Furthermore, when we look more closely within the community we see clearly how factors such as education, type of employment, and level of income make a difference in marriageable mates and the stability of marriage.

There exists compelling evidence that African American women who are poor are less likely to be married. African American men who come from poor or economically marginalized families and communities are at a greater risk of dropping out of school, remaining unemployed, and entering the criminal justice system. Thus the grave dilemma of black male incarceration. There have been reports indicating that a staggering 30 percent of all African American men are in jail, on parole, or on probation. *The New York Times,* in an April 26, 2000, front-page article, reported that minorities, especially blacks, are overrepresented at all phases of the juvenile justice process. Blacks are more than six times as likely as whites to be sentenced to prison by juvenile courts. This by itself creates a condition of male absence from the community.

Dissatisfaction with formal education and unacceptable employment opportunities have driven more African American males out of schools, albeit unprepared for the workforce, where they are frequently underemployed or unemployed. The immediate rewards of illicit activities, such as peddling drugs, lure many. The sad outcome of this is a climate where violence and fratricide are a major health risk for African American men. Black men engaged in unlawful employment are competing for the narrow window of opportunities to feel in control of a situation that brings significance to personal identity, but at devastating costs.

HIV and other preventable physical and mental health risks are decimating the pool of potential mates. Nor can you ignore the number of African American men unavailable to African American women because of homosexuality. If an African American woman insists on a set of standards for mate selection, she must apply them to an ever-shrinking pool of eligible men.

The situation becomes even more complicated for highly educated women. The more education a woman has, the more difficult it is to find an available mate with comparable or better career possibilities. Paul Glick, in Harriette McAdoo's book, *Black Families,* reports that "black female college graduates are less likely to marry, or to remarry if divorced, than their less-educated counterparts, both black and white." This situation also gives eligible black men additional leverage should they desire to play the field.

Conversely, African American men with college or advanced degrees select from a wider pool of acceptable women—a pool that includes black women with less education, as well as women from other ethnic groups. On the other hand, Staples and Johnson report that "in ninety-eight percent of marriages with a black bride, the groom will be a black male."

Ambivalence in black women about the success of relationships with African American men is tied to the increasingly prevalent concern over an inability to depend on black men. In contrast, a black man's doubt about success in a relationship is tied to anxiety about feeling "trapped," or the ability to establish a presence in the relationship that results in self-respect and dignity. The male–female gender ratio difference provides black men with more opportunity to treat any given relationship lightly. Thus they question the necessity to persevere through difficult periods, thereby contributing to instability in partnerships.

Clearly, the vast majority of African American men do not worry about finding an acceptable mate in the same fashion as do African American women. One of the important benefits of the large pool of acceptable women from which an African American man can select is the option to find a mate who will support his view of himself, and the behavior he adopts to combat the invisibility syndrome.

Joe and Sharita—Commitment Based on Convenience

It was during a consultation with the son of Joe's new partner, Sharita, that it became apparent that his commitment to the relationship was one of convenience. Sharita asked Joe to help with her ten-year-old, who had begun to display behavioral problems in school. Joe's reluctance to "do anything" frustrated Sharita. Joe felt justified in his hands-off atti-tude. It was not his son. "His *own* father should be involved," Joe be-lieved. Although disappointed, Sharita understood. She was under-standing of Joe in many ways.

Dependent upon food stamps and welfare, stressed out over the dif-ficulty in finding employment, Sharita nevertheless accepts Joe's tran-sient presence in her home and his constant unemployment. Ironically, she is supporting Joe emotionally and financially. When Joe launches into "it's tough on a black man" tirades, Sharita is a real "amen cor-ner," as she expresses her very sympathetic attitude toward his views. This is what Joe likes most about her. "She understands me," he says.

Still, angry confrontations occur when money is in short supply. Whenever Sharita challenges Joe's lack of financial contribution, the fireworks begin. If she speaks her mind and says, "You use the black man's problem to bitch and moan because you can't deliver," he becomes physically abusive. When I asked Sharita why she puts up with the situation, she said, "He isn't that bad most of the time, and he does help me with my children once in a while. And he's fun when we go out."

For Joe, Sharita creates a haven from the discontent and disappointments bred of his inability to acquire a way of life free of what he perceives as "injustices for the black man." Her compliance helps quell and purge his internal demons. In Sharita, he has found acceptance and a precious brand of nurturance. She will take him back, comfort him, and nurse his psychological wounds. She is "there for me," he explains. Her behavior bestows stature upon him. Her support verifies his significance. On the other hand, "just being there" is Joe's biggest contribution.

Joe and Sharita are not unique. They have found usefulness and convenience in the arrangements of their relationship. They have meshed psychologically in a complementary fashion. Their needs for companionship and sexual intimacy are fulfilled. Sharita may have hopes—not an expectation—that Joe will one day help more with the finances and the children. But Sharita would rather endure unfulfilled expectations than to risk not having a man around at all, and she has settled for Joe.

Sharita's attraction to Joe is firmly anchored in his looks and "how he can talk." Joe dresses smartly and handles himself with style. Sharita loves his flair and confidence in dealing with the brothers on the street, or in the nightclubs when they go out partying. When he has money in his pocket—sometimes just hers—he is lavish in his spending on her.

In his element, Joe has an engaging visibility that aggrandizes his identity. His more carefree attitude compensates for Sharita's tight-fisted, worrisome style. Joe is something that many of her woman friends do not have—a man. Although they frown on how he occasionally mistreats her, they view having a man around most of the time as an attractive alternative to their singleness. Sharita is Joe's "fine mama." She is a real looker. Brothers' heads turn when she passes. Together, Joe and Sharita come close to the partnership they both desire. Despite the relationship's shortcomings, in their view it offers a companionship that is far superior to being alone.

No matter what others' opinions may be about its appropriateness, Joe and Sharita have found in their relationship intrinsic elements to help them "feel important" and "to be together." They have established a mutual ground of met needs, even though "making the best out of a bad situation" may lead into predicaments that prove ultimately self-destructive.

Making the best out of any difficult situation clearly implies focusing on the positive things in your life—counting your blessings—as a necessary salve for having so little. Such themes have been one of the lessons embedded in the blues, the musical form that has chronicled African American life for generations. We know that many single female-headed households have men as part of the family system and larger social network. Joe and Sharita's alliance is an example of that. But it is apparent that constructive participation and leadership in the family and home by African American men is on the decline. This sad fact, however, does not stop African American couples from entering into relationships with traditional expectations that the man will fulfill the role of head-of-household and breadwinner. It does not diminish women's expectations of parenting help.

Despite gender-driven differences in expectations, according to Billingsley, "sixty-two percent of African American adults indicate that both partners benefit about equally from their relationships."

Black Male Sexism and Black Female Independence

In these changing times, a dominating male posture in male-female relationships is increasingly considered unacceptable behavior. Black women are among the first to point out that to be powerful at another's expense is neither workable nor acceptable—so there exists a deep-seated problem for black men attempting to maintain traditional male roles.

When I counsel couples, I see men trying to control the tenor of communication between themselves and their partners. When disagreements occur they very likely will be interpreted as challenges to the way the man has crafted his image and sense of self, or how he has gained his stature. He must now protect his dignity and self-respect—sometimes at all costs. But because his provocateur in this instance is his wife or girlfriend, he must restrain himself.

The code of the brotherhood dictates that a man, as Joe puts it, "don't take no shit off a woman." These ideas about black manhood can turn into the mentality so tragically and fatally represented in so many of our urban street youth. Although many African American men know, on some level, the street code of behavior that's to be employed when disrespected, and grapple with managing it, they are particularly at odds with themselves when provoked by black women. The vast majority do not react with the violence of some of our urban youth, nor do they resort to physical attacks. But "up in your face" challenges by a black woman to a black male's views (or a discrediting of how he's achieving) can be fanned into intense internal frustrations and volatile skirmishes.

The African American man is taught not to tolerate effrontery and disrespectful behavior. There is an expectation that a man will display appropriate indignation and intolerance of disrespect. When a certain line is crossed, there is always the literal and figurative solution, "Let's take it outside." Contributing further to the black man's internal conflict about how to respond to his confrontational partner is his desire for her to nurture him. The nurturing role black women play in the lives of black men often reflects the nourishing roles played by our mothers. The pleasure-pain, love-hate that developed out of that relationship can spill over into subsequent relationships with women. Likewise, the kind of experiences black women have had with their fathers—his loving and supportive ways, her idealized fantasies created around an absent father, emotional distortions that come out of a father's abuse, or their experiences in relationships with other men—can shape how they respond to their current partners. Certainly, we black men and women are students of what peers and elders taught us about the "goodness" in relationships with each other. In the field of psychology, it is axiomatic that a man's relationship to his mother in part determines his selection of and subsequent ties to his partner. This psychological dynamic shapes the response of the man to any challenge from her.

It is ironic that many African American mothers, while raising their black male children, encourage their sons to respond with indignation when they encounter slights. Joe, Bill, Jim, and Sam all recall occasions when their mothers pushed them to be assertive when mistreated. Many black mothers have also made efforts to teach their sons how to treat a woman. The behavior they expect their sons to exhibit toward women is very often influenced by their own history of treatment by the men in their lives. At the same time sons are admonished to be "smart" in choosing their battles and standing up for their dignity, black parents punish sassiness at home. Even if children are justifiably indignant, uncontested obedience is still a primary expectation among African American parents. It is in this light that African American men place considerable importance on protecting their love relationships from becoming yet another battlefield.

Joe placed significant importance upon Sharita's compliance with his thinking. This desire for like-mindedness also characterized his relationship with his buddies at the club. Having people listen to him and stand in alliance with his positions was prime to Joe's sense of power.

Unfortunately, Joe's jobs were a wasteland when it came to the support of his view of the world. Many times in the workplace the climate of racial intolerance was not even masked, as Joe was subjected to demeaning racial jokes and comments. Therefore, the private world he created with Sharita was a very precious place to amplify his dignity and self-respect. Joe was understandably intolerant when he perceived Sharita (or anyone, or anything) as tampering with the safe haven he had created.

Fragile Egos

It sometimes appears that black male pride is easily hurt by superficial circumstances. If our reactions at first glance appear unwarranted, look for the reason in our mistreatment, somewhere, at some time, and at some place, by someone.

As Earl talked with his wife, Ann, about his indignation with the school psychologist, the conversation began to escalate into an argument. Ann accused Earl of overreacting and of rudeness.

"You could have been nicer and handled it better," she complained. However, Earl felt he had done a remarkable job of calming himself down from a rage of wanting to "hit the b———." At one point Earl had moved forward menacingly, planting himself directly in the teacher's line of vision saying, "Excuse me, may I say something?" His wife, Ann, was mortified by this behavior. She felt that Earl came across as unnecessarily brutish. Furthermore, the impression he made could jeopardize their son's relationship with school authorities. Ann felt they might think, "Like father, like son." "I didn't want that image conveyed," she admitted.

For Ann to chastise him made Earl feel misunderstood. That special emotional intimacy she always claimed to have seemed hollow. It put her avowals of "I know where you are coming from," in a category that Earl saw as "serving her own purpose to manipulate situations between the two of us." Ann's claims of emotional intimacy were tarnished by Earl's growing belief that this intimacy was deliberately used as a tactic to "keep me in check, not to understand me."

When Bill told his wife, Gloria, of his mistreatment in the restaurant, she related her similar experiences, spinning her opinion of how he should have reacted to this encounter. "She didn't listen," Bill lamented. What Bill meant was that Gloria rarely tunes into the background music in his life. "She never looks at the big picture, only at what stands out," Bill complained in a very annoyed tone. A native of the old South, Gloria had heard many stories of the legion of indignities suffered by her relatives and friends. It was not such a big thing to her, and she fully expected Bill to handle it. She saw him as an educated, prominent, upwardly mobile professional who knew that these things happen. "You should not let them get to you" was her advice.

Of course, part of what operated in Gloria's unconscious was an unspoken apprehension that there may come a time when some indignity becomes the straw that breaks the camel's back—sending Bill into protracted self-doubt and depression, leading him into immobility, rendering him unable to work. Although she has never seen him respond in this way, it is her private fear. This was the unfortunate circumstance of several men in her extended family, whose paralysis created tragic situations. Bill's anger over his mistreatment was intensified by what he considered to be Gloria's insensitivity to the meaning he attached to the situation. It was colored by hurt, disillusionment, and confusion. He did not want to appear vulnerable in the eyes of his children. The restaurant episode exposed the fact that he was not as powerful and in control of things as he would like to have them believe. He wanted to show his son, in particular, that he could handle situations of both subtle and blatant discrimination, thus reinforcing his dignity by being a proper paternal role model. But Bill felt this incident deeply tainted his image as the teacher of family lessons, and his ability to hand down a legacy of handling racial encounters.

It is always important to Bill's personal identity to be seen as a wise family elder. Gloria allowed her assumptions about his being "a strong man" and her "ways of doing things" to cloud her recognition of his upset and disgust. But she did not see her behavior this way. In fact, she believed that she was shoring up Bill's self-esteem by playing down the encounter as the "normal" travails of African Americans. For Gloria, his handling of the situation in no way diminished him—which she considered the most important thing to convey to Bill at the time. On the other hand, she admitted being surprised by Bill's response, since he is usually more restrained.

Gloria felt that her inability to connect emotionally to Bill's upset was a casualty of their hectic work schedules. They talk frequently about the discrimination and prejudice in the country, but not enough about what really troubles them personally. They have an unspoken motivation in common to be sure to stay ahead of the forces of racism—as Ann says, "trying to keep racism in its place." That's why they work so hard.

Black Men's Reaction Formation: "Hate the One You Love"

As I have stressed throughout this book, the pressures on African American men are immense. In our persistent out-of-the-mainstream position that is so greatly aggravated by dominant problems of unemployment and incarceration, there seems to be no dry ground upon which to stand and build respect. Even for those significant numbers of African American men who are contributing to family and community, the negatives overshadow their noble efforts.

By eating away at the psychological cement of black male self-esteem, invisibility is continuously creating mixed and unstable feelings of confidence and mastery. The resulting abuse—verbal and physical—that African American men direct toward African American women is a direct result of the constant flux of our psychological makeup. Challenges to our sense of self, and manipulations of our vulnerabilities—particularly those we feel are by-products of "black male oppression"—inevitably are provocative. What provokes us may be a superficial narcissistic injury—our pride gets hurt. The unfortunate follow-up to our hurt pride is to "get up in your face," and black women, as well as other brothers, become our likely targets.

Another troubling response for black men is to shut down, walk away, and indulge in a smoldering sulk. Withdrawal and isolation is a common form of coping with conflict. Our silence allows us to repress anger that we are afraid to express. This is especially true when we fear going out of control in dealings with our wife or girlfriend.

I believe that under some of the anger, volatility, and tension in our aggressive interactions with African American women may be the psychological defense mechanism called reaction formation. Reaction formation, as defined in the *American Psychiatric Glossary,* operates unconsciously, allowing the person to adopt affects, ideas, attitudes, and behaviors that are the opposite of impulses he or she harbors, consciously or unconsciously. For example, on some level many African American men find themselves struggling with love and admiration for African American women's fabled capacity to be resilient and strong, regardless of what racism throws at them. Reaction formation is exhibiting behavior that opposes those feelings. For example, the maternal attachments formed during child rearing have shown African American women how to use family to give purpose and to ease the stress that comes from suffering inequities. But African American men have not found roles in the family to serve them with empowerment in quite the same way. The life-and-death issues that exist in child raising have evolved into a greater priority for black women than the sole struggle against racism.

Blocked by the invisibility syndrome, we do not celebrate and affirm how such strength informs our judgments about life. Nor are we willing to acknowledge and lean on black women's wisdom. Instead, we repress the lessons to be learned from African American women, transforming even those learned from our mothers. To heed female lessons about resiliency challenges our sense of male leadership. This reaction is formed because such acknowledgment or admiration is too psychologically painful, and it potentially exposes our failings and the insecurities that flow from them. Given the virulence of racism, which is so intertwined with sexism, we feel that we cannot afford to have learned our roles from the "weaker sex." In the face of a consistently denigrating societal climate, it is a matter of pride and self-respect.

As you can see, racism and sexism are agents of the invisibility syndrome that make recognizing and learning from the strengths of African American women psychologically difficult for black men. Therefore, some of the tension between African American men and women is a reaction formation, manifested unconsciously as "hate the one you love."

Black Women's Reaction Formation: "Love the One You Hate"

African American women, too, bring their own form of reaction formation to relationships with black men. That dynamic can take the underlying and unspoken form of "love the one you hate." Such an unconscious sentiment has developed for some women out of their resiliency. Hardships have hardened them against the vagaries of life. They have learned to cope with or without a man. Mothers may struggle to teach their sons how to be resilient, but as role models they are intrinsically more suitable to instruct their daughters.

As female-headed single-parent households become the majority in the African American community, black daughters remain immersed in an appropriate gender context, surrounded by mother, grandmother, aunts, godmothers, and girlfriends. The women around them reinforce the gender messages black mothers convey to their daughters. Unfortunately, these mothers cannot socialize their sons with such home-based role models, because of the profound inaccessibility of black fathers and men. This circumstance has led black mothers to prepare their daughters to be even more resilient and self-reliant. They are taught to pursue dreams that grow from the wisdom of the women around them. The traditional expectations of marriage and partnership cannot be taken for granted. As one woman put it, "It would be stupid and unproductive for black women to prepare their girls to be dependent upon black men, given their economic and social conditions."

The doubt and disappointments that pit the terrain of a relationship with black men can strain the love. Although black women may at first identify with and be empathetic toward the difficulty facing men, on some level they feel disdain for the man's "not getting it together." But this feeling toward someone you are supposed to love can be too painful, too unacceptable. The racial superego says, "As an African American woman, you should not disrespect African American men—your own people! Is this not what they are constantly experiencing in the larger world? Are not such feelings a form of racial self-hatred?" Entangled in this horrendous dichotomy, black women opt not to disrespect themselves; instead, they become intolerant of, and at times feel hatred for, the machinations of black masculinity. African American women should ask themselves if their acts of love and indulgence of African American men are overcompensating for the contempt they feel for their husband's or boyfriend's lack of leadership, either in the home, in the community, or both.

Most African American women have an enduring hope for African American men, even though at times it gasps under the stranglehold of bitter disappointments. But the love between us persists. The attachment continues, if only because each mother knows that every man was once a mother's son. This insight is the wisdom and the message behind "Mother to Son," by Langston Hughes, a favorite poem of mine:

Well, son, I'll tell you:
Life for me ain't been no crystal stair.
It's had tacks in it,
And splinters,
And boards torn up,
And places with no carpet on the floor—
Bare.
But all the time
I'se been a-climbin' on
And reachin' landin's
And turnin' corners,
And sometimes goin' in the dark
Where there ain't been no light.
So boy, don't you turn back.
Don't you set down on the steps
'Cause you finds it's kinder hard.
Don't you fall now—
For I'se still goin', honey,
I'se
still climbin',
And life for me ain't been no crystal stair.

I also believe men can learn to listen and change. One day I bumped into Joe by accident walking across the street in the neighborhood of my office with a little girl. She turned out to be one of Sharita's children. I asked how that relationship was going. He looked at me and held up the child's hand.

"Picking her up regularly from school now, does that answer your question?"

I was surprised, but not completely, given my memory of the contentious but yet enmeshed nature of their relationship.

"Still have my demons though," Joe said.

PART FOUR

MOVING ON: FROM BROTHERHOOD TO MANHOOD

The tragedy of life doesn't lie in not reaching your goal. The tragedy lies in having no goal to reach. It isn't a calamity to die with dreams unfulfilled, but it is a calamity not to dream. It is not a disaster to be unable to capture your ideal, but it is a disaster to have no ideal to capture. It is not a disgrace not to reach the stars, but it is a disgrace to have no stars to reach for.

—Dr. Benjamin Mays, former president of Morehouse College

9

SEEKING HELP: TRUSTING THE WISDOM OF OTHERS

The Dilemma of Always Showing Strength

"Be your own man," D. J. said to Rod with authority as they sipped beer on the front steps. The other guys around him nodded approvingly. The suggestion behind this thinking is far reaching: You are not much of a man if you let another take advantage of you, and you are not much of a man if you need help. Brotherhood exists to support your ability to be your own man with contentious, unbridled enthusiasm.

You have seen that that way of thinking is a significant part of our upbringing. We are taught to be our own men as we silently wage our personal struggles against those negative forces that single us out. We learn from the brotherhood code how to run life's gauntlet without admitting any weakness. Failure to achieve any of our goals can mean someone or something has gotten the better of us. It means there were barriers we could not get around. When we fail, we wonder: Is it because of not being a good enough man, because of being black, or both?

By not surmounting that way of thinking we miss the chance to understand our human frailties. By ignoring the fact that help can be essential to our achievements we overlook the fact that solving our problems may very well start by simply reaching out.

Frank and Jackie

Frank finally admitted to his support group that he and Jackie had broken up. She accused him of not being serious about their relationship, and cited his poor money management as an example. Instead of saving for their wedding and other things they had agreed to sacrifice for, Frank always came up with excuses. He continued to buy expensive clothes and what Jackie called his expensive toys, like the new stereo sound system. Jackie felt that Frank always wanted to impress people, particularly his boys, and that he put that above his relationship with her, as he did with others in the past. She loved him, but she advised him to get some help about his "thing" with money. Frank didn't appreciate that and he copped an attitude.

Jackie hadn't known that Frank had borrowed heavily from relatives, friends, and others. And now they were demanding payment on their loans. Frank was big into appearances, which made reaching out for help difficult, if not impossible. He still resisted the idea of telling Jackie the truth.

Chuck and Jock

Chuck tugged at his pants and coat as he got into his walk leaving his probation officer's desk. Passing other brothers waiting for their appointments, he caught their eyes and gave that knowing nod, signaling that they all were only putting up with this shit and couldn't wait to get out of there. Chuck, like many others waiting in the office, would light up a blunt—a fat marijuana joint—only blocks away from the building, get a little mellow from a few hits, and then blend back into street life.

Today, however, was different. Halfway out the door, Chuck turned around and headed back to his probation officer's desk. When he got to the desk he admitted to his startled probation officer that he could not read and that he wanted help to get into a reading program. Jock, an older brother and experienced former gangbanger, had talked to

Chuck about turning his life around. Those conversations were behind Chuck's decision.

Recognizing the Need for Help

What is important to us is sometimes based on what we think is important to others, particularly when it involves maintaining an image. Frank and Chuck each had his image to consider when deciding to reach out for help. Frank seemed to be puzzled by his girlfriend Jackie's advice about seeking help. This made her comments even more disturbing to him, since he did not see any truth to her warnings. And her frank comments that he didn't have it together made him question her true support, and therefore her love for him.

Chuck, on the other hand, thought about Jock's advice. Jock was in his ear constantly with warnings about his fate if he didn't turn away from street life. Jock used his life as an example to make his case to Chuck. Chuck respected Jock; he believed Jock had his best interest in mind and meant him no harm. In fact, Jock was one of few persons he knew who truly felt that he could amount to something more than a thug. Jock had credibility with Chuck, and so he thought about what he had to say.

Both Frank and Chuck had to accept the credibility of the person delivering the message to them. The difference in the way each handled the information was due to how it impacted his self-image. Both had worked hard to carve out a particular image that made them feel important. They had, in this success, overcome feeling invisible, and had become surefooted with personal confidence. To change further meant journeying down new paths of discovery, relying on not only themselves but others as well. To reach out for help, particularly from others, was uncharacteristic, scary, and uncomfortable.

Like Frank and Chuck, we find ways to regulate our daily routines with some certainty, in order to cope with internal conflict, confusion, and self-doubt. Our instincts tell us to hold onto these familiar ways. To break the hold of the familiar requires courage. It also requires breaking out of the macho bravado trap.

Our rules promote the competitive "one-upmanship, cover-your-ass game" as the attitude necessary for individual success. Since there are significant competitive tensions and self-destructive tendencies among African American men, self-reliance becomes a safer alternative to soliciting the help of other black men. To ask for help is to disclose weakness, and it makes one vulnerable. Black men cannot appear weak to female or male partners, to family, to friends, or to the community.

These are personal attributes that "real" brothers reject. To seek help with problems threatens to weaken the foundation of what we have chiseled out as our position in our community, as well as what image we want to be projected to the white community.

Negative Lessons from the Workplace

In the work environment the caution of black men toward solving problems and seeking help is further reinforced. We learn that we must carefully weigh how we divulge our uncertainties and troubles, much less our options to solve them. This is particularly true for difficulties that we may have in competently performing our job. The work culture presumes acceptable competence upon hiring, and that personal growth and our mastery of job skills will continue to be demonstrated. Many African American men think carefully about how they should initiate requests for assistance, or disclose difficulty in a work environment, in order to preserve their chances of recognition, raises, and promotions. If such disclosures are warmly received and encouraged in a supportive manner it facilitates competency development. On the other hand, there is enough skepticism from our personal experiences to know that this kind of reception is quite often not forthcoming, and can be deceptive if and when extended. Too many of us have followed the rules in the spirit of the work environment, only to learn that they can be applied differently to us. Consequently, inclinations to seek help for a problem on the job can be compromised by concern about how it will reflect on our competency, and perhaps impact stereotypical notions about black men.

The Burden of Proof: James's Story

James had worked as a mixer in a chemical plant for a number of years. He got the job right out of high school, and he desired to continue his education and pursue a college degree when he saved enough money to return to school. He very much wanted to succeed at this job and impress his supervisor. He understood as well that one's supervisor has great influence over promotions and pay raises.

James was the only black male on his work team, and he noticed that whenever they were given assignments his supervisor would take a little extra time with him to make sure he understood. He found this just a little condescending, since he had no difficulty grasping new responsibilities. However, he understood his supervisor's concern that his performance would be part of how the work team's efforts were viewed by management. Being targeted in this way made James self-conscious as well as reluctant and cautious about asking questions when tasks were unclear. Moreover, his supervisor's overly attentive attitude toward his performance caused the other members of his team to worry that their performance record might hinge entirely on his performance. It also made James fear that his work record would influence attitudes about black job-seekers in the future. Whereas his other coworkers could easily approach the supervisor with questions, James was uncertain of how he would be perceived for doing the same.

The dilemma James found himself in is not uncommon for black men. Asking questions and obtaining clarifications in order to do one's job well is common in the workplace. Yet, when seeking help is linked to an extraordinary burden of proof—proof that one is competent above the usual expectations—then the manner in which help is requested requires extraordinary tact. It also becomes another personal lesson in how to solve problems and seek help. This is how the proverb "You have to be twice as good in order to get half as much" becomes the rule in the African American community. The anger produced by these workplace encounters promotes an avoidance of seeking help. That avoidance keeps us from learning the value of seeking timely help that facilitates growth and development.

What Goes on Within—What Employers Need to Know

How do black men solve life problems, and to whom do we go for help, advice, and solace when we confront intransigent societal structures that are unwilling to meaningfully include us? How do we decide to adjust (or to sacrifice) our sense of pride for a future good—believing, for example, that taking a menial job in the end will lead to a better opportunity or a better outcome? Who will we tell how it feels to accept a position that is beneath our sense of self? And how do we share what it feels like to be part of a continuing legacy of African American men getting less out of life than do white men of the same class? There are too many examples of how starting from the bottom—which is part of our world of work—has only gradually led African American men to the proverbial "next higher rung"—a rung still very far from the ladder's top.

Most of all, African American men cannot allow themselves to appear to have capitulated to prejudice and discrimination by succumbing to the frustrations and denigration it creates. In the tradition of the credo "When the going gets tough, the tough get going," the going is always tough for African American men. Under these conditions, and within this frame of mind, it is not reasonable to expect us to ask for help or show that we need it.

Early Lessons in Learning about Making Decisions: Matt's Story

Ten-year-old Matt entered the classroom prepared for any questions the teacher asked the class. Matt was rarely called upon, although he was frequently ready. His raised hand was consistently overlooked. When he was acknowledged, his answers never seemed quite acceptable, and he noticed that the teacher often asked the same questions of one of his white or black female classmates, who responded apparently more to the teacher's liking. He never got the same knowing nod and smile as they did. Many of his buddies reported similar experiences. In time, he didn't raise his hand as much anymore, because he knew his teacher would not call upon him for his unsatisfactory answers.

Matt was learning that how he interacted with the teacher made a difference in his classroom recognition. The less active he was in engaging the learning process, the more attention he drew to himself. He also learned that it was not what he knew that got attention as much as how he behaved. He soon learned that his answers were used as a poor performance standard to which his classmates could compare more favorably. So he learned, to not be embarrassed, don't raise your hand.

What so often happens in the school setting for African American children is that asking for help is a risk. It often ends negatively.

Step-by-Step into the Invisibility Trap—Recognizing the Red Flags

What this circumstance does is set us up for a pattern of step-by-step experiences that continue our powerlessness, confusion, and disillusionment through isolation, and thus invisibility, by creating an inability to capture a sense of feeling like a genuine participator. It works its way into the heart and mind by a sequence of events that pushes each one of us toward greater isolation.

1. **Minimal recognition in many everyday situations** often gets translated by us as an environment of disrespect for African American men, and it is further interpreted as rejection or dismissal, especially in times of personal need.

2. **Rejection and dismissal** triggers a "fuck it" macho male arrogance to "go it alone," or a retaliatory act to regain self-respect, honor, and dignity.

3. **Going it alone** means solving problems in isolation.

4. **Isolation** voids the benefit of supports and makes us more dependent upon self-reliance for validation of personal experiences and accomplishments.

5. **More reliance on self-validated experiences** further isolates, breeding suspicion, paranoia, and less receptivity to acknowledgment from others.

6. **Repeated experiences of total self-reliance** nurture the development of a dysfunctional person—one who is destined to believe he is "terminally unique"—that "no one else has my kind of problems."

7. **Terminally unique thinking** impacts problem solving and seeking help by cutting one off from other possibilities for tackling problems and seeing value in group support. It does this by convincing us that personal needs must be hidden or invisible in order to maintain respect and dignity.

8. A constant, terminally unique view of the world, or total dependence upon self-reliance, can lead to **racism survivor burnout,** leading us to succumb to our frustrations about finding solutions to overcoming prejudice and discrimination. Disappointments immerse us deeper into disillusionment and confusion—the symptoms of the invisibility syndrome.

Doing It on Your Own: How "Terminally Unique" Strategies Keep Us from Seeking Help

Terminally unique strategies employed to solve problems and to avoid seeking help play into a legacy of mistrust. Likewise, the inability to disclose weaknesses and solicit advice as a means of strengthening one's self is in keeping with black male issues about power and control. There is great reluctance to put confidence in others, since integrity and trust has been compromised so much in the past. But, for us to continue an individualistic orientation to life decisions is to lose the counsel and wisdom of others who might very well know of a better way. A lack of consultation with others promotes not just decision making in isolation, but breeds personal arrogance, emotional distance from, and contempt for others.

Invisibility preys upon isolation, and it becomes the "I'll take care of myself" attitude. It works against achieving the kind of cohesion and cooperation necessary to develop constructive partnerships within our families, workplaces, and community. It also supports the antagonistic behavior of not letting someone "get the best of you," a tenet for proving your manhood. It is the face-saving imperative of "equalizing" the relationship, or bringing the person down to the same, if not lower level than you, that is the problem.

How Racial Identity or Race Consciousness Affects Our Willingness to Receive Help

Our own race consciousness and racial identity can also determine our reactions to receiving help. One poignant example of this is a story told to me by a friend of Brother Akim, an outspoken African American community activist who experienced chest pains one day and was rushed to the hospital.

When Brother Akim got to the hospital, his anxiety about his physical condition was exacerbated by how he thought the doctors would view him. His activism not only had caused him to confront many of the institutions in the community—challenging their discriminatory practices—but it also had immersed him deeply into an African-centered world view. As a child of the old segregated South and a student of life conditions for African Americans, he knew that health care and medical treatment in certain hospitals were inadequate, if not unethical, when it came to black people. On the way to the hospital, he also thought about how his medical condition made him helpless, and would put him at the mercy of white doctors. The thought of this made him so distraught that his behavior deteriorated into hysteria, extreme agitation, and explosive ranting that bordered on a paranoid psychotic episode. Brother Akim's delusions made him fear reprisal for his activist stands from those entrusted to provide his medical care.

Mixed Messages

The African American family and community collude in an interesting way with the manner in which African American men approach problem-solving and seeking help. On the one hand, the family and community want black men to be effective solvers of life problems, especially when it enhances quality of life for the family and community. On the other hand, in fulfilling that expectation there is awareness that African American men showing such competency and leadership is risky in the larger society. Society seems to tolerate only the success of a few, not the black majority. To take charge of your life requires taking control of your personal circumstances, such as being assertive about self-interests, and engaging institutions, policies, and practices that deny opportunities. When we take leadership in this fashion, however, we get mixed messages from the family and community. On the one hand they promote individual efficacy, but on the other hand this same behavior is tempered by family cautions, because of racism's tendency to dampen, if not eliminate, any threatening rise in black male power and leadership.

I think of the example of Mike Espy of Mississippi, a political rising star who was appointed U.S. Secretary of Agriculture by President Clinton. Shortly after that appointment he was accused of improprieties in a conflict-of-interest investigation. His appointment was cut short, overwhelmed by accusations and the need to defend himself. After many years of investigation, disruption to his personal and political life, and a damaged reputation, Mike Espy was exonerated.

Then there is Billie, an assistant to the butcher in a supermarket chain. He raised concerns about the quality of the meat being sold to consumers who were "captive customers," given the lack of stores in his inner-city neighborhood. His alarm caused other black employees to voice their concerns about the quality of the food products delivered to this community store. Two weeks after Billie made this an issue, he got a pink slip for not meeting the standards of a butcher's assistant. His family told him to keep his mouth shut the next time.

When you talk to black men about these examples, many cannot help but attribute gender and race as the motive behind such treatment. The reactions to these two stories demonstrate how quickly African Americans conclude that society is intolerant of black men being out front and outspoken, or equally, wheeling and dealing in the same backyard as white men. Many believe that we must be careful of how we conduct ourselves, while still needing to take personal risks in order to get ahead.

Overcoming Fears of Asking for Help

It is essential for African American men to learn how to lean upon and rely on each other for wisdom and strength, if we are going to rectify the conditions of our family and community life. Using each other as resources is an important step in that direction.

Too often we feel overwhelmed by the magnitude of problems about being black and being male, and we feel unable to do anything. Once again, this is how the invisibility syndrome dispenses confusion, sowing internal messages like, "Oh, it's horrible to play this race card business," or "It's not as bad as it is made out to be," or "I don't have a problem—and what can I do, anyway?"

Thinking that "I must be a big leader," or "I must do something great" gets in the way of solving our problems. We are blind to seeing small steps as legitimate efforts. Each of us must think of our contributions as only one piece of a larger picture, a greater plan that may or may not be realized in our lifetime. No effort is too small. However, we elect to remain alone, grappling with private feelings that say no one appreciates or understands us.

We must decide if our gratification can be deferred and if our present efforts can be an investment in the future. Much of the disrespect shown by the young toward us as elders is born of their feeling that we, as adult African Americans, have not provided a better life for them. We have not freed them from injustices and racism. This is why helping and being helped toward a common goal for a common good must become an intrinsic value.

The identity of different groups over generations—whether it's the Xhosa of South Africa, the Palestinians, the Serbs, the Sioux, the Irish, the Israelis, or various ethnic groups of Americans in the United States—is built upon a cultural history. Having a sense of it gives substance and purpose to their efforts and longevity to their identity. We as African American men must learn from history that change comes slowly. But it won't come at all if there's no clear vision or effort toward a common goal. Frederick Douglass's famous line that "power concedes nothing without a demand" can be understood as a personal challenge to each black man, that there can be no self-empowerment without demands being put first upon ourselves. Moreover, we must understand that the self-empowered person cannot prosper unless others also prosper from *our* self-empowerment. Inevitably, we must decide what we are willing to sacrifice and what we are willing to commit to individually and collectively that will result in changing conditions in our lives, in our families, and in our communities.

10

THE TWELVE LESSONS OF EMPOWERMENT

Lesson Number One: Know the Deal and Be Prepared

What factors contribute to success, peace, and happiness? Opportunity, education, money, and luck are at the top of most people's lists. Here are some prerequisites for pulling all those factors together:

- Be honest about your motivation
- Know your strengths and weaknesses
- Admit your weaknesses
- Gain appropriate knowledge and skill
- Confront problems openly
- Confront symptoms of invisibility that hold you back
- Invest personal time in your goals
- Use ingenuity and creativity to identify possibilities where supposedly there are none
- Work on your attitude and personality
- Learn interpersonal people skills

I see my clients' personal power emerge when they realize that every one of these prerequisites is within their grasp. History has already proven our courage. Everyday I see further evidence of the courage of black men who are facing obstacles, finding alternatives, and persisting despite discouragement. Future generations will undoubtedly look back and reflect on how courageous this generation was, too.

Lesson Number Two: Take Advice from Our Elders

A book I discovered recently tells of the unheralded courage of common folks. In *Roads from the Bottom,* C. K. Chiplin recounts his father's tenacity and faith making the best of every day, surviving acts of racism that were meant to break the spirit, but thriving nevertheless— raising eight children in Marcus Bottom, Vicksburg, Mississippi, always demonstrating how proud he was to be black and how he was willing to die for the cause of freedom. James Chiplin Sr. died in 1992, well into his eighties, but he and his wife, Rosa, left behind their personal wisdom for all to follow:

- First Road: Know Yourself
- Second Road: Respect Yourself and Others
- Third Road: Faith
- Fourth Road: A Good Education
- Fifth Road: Never Give Up
- Sixth Road: Associate with People Who Are Trying to Advance
- Seventh Road: Help Somebody Else
- Eighth Road: Stand Up for Something
- Ninth Road: Trust in God
- Tenth Road: Pray

James and Rosa Chiplin succeeded in life because they were resilient, had a dream about family, and worked to make it happen. They were empowered. They figured out how to make life work for themselves, and, as a testimony of their compassion for us, left their pearls of wisdom. This is an act of empowering, sharing with others. It is another important trait of empowerment.

The Chiplins' pearls of wisdom are deceptively simple, but complex in their fulfillment. I challenge you to think, reflect awhile upon each one, and explore what it would take to journey completely down each road with self-integrity. We should not take the Chiplins' advice lightly; they have lived it and have something to show for it. That is credibility.

Lesson Number Three: Find Your Internal Compass

To accomplish self-empowerment on whatever roads we choose to travel, we must look inward. Existing personal resources are the foundation of our own self-motivation and the drive toward competency, excellence, and vision. Consider Ted's story.

Ted had been out of prison for a year and out of a drug program for six months. Staying clean was important if he was to reestablish a relationship with his thirteen-year-old son, whose mother warned Ted that he was in the streets and headed down the same path as he. By twenty-eight he had been in and out of jail for half of his life, he nearly overdosed twice, and finally flirted with the Nation of Islam his last time in prison. They helped him get discipline, find self-pride, and discover a purpose in life. He goes to the mosque occasionally, but now believes he has a mission in helping youth to stay out of trouble and avoid his pitfalls. He has volunteered as an addiction counselor in a youth center during the day, works in a warehouse at night, and is thinking about returning to school. He wants to learn how to be a more effective counselor to save the drug-using brothers and sisters on the streets.

Ted did more than find outlets for creating a self-image that merely defies what others believe about him. He did more than dispatch self-doubts and disillusionment. He rose above all of this by acquiring a type of self-motivation and resiliency that was dedicated not only to changing conditions in his life but the lives of those around him as well. He set realistic goals within a personal vision of high standards. An internal compass of values accurately pointed him in the right direction.

Lesson Number Four: Get Past Feeling Embarrassed

Bill was one of the first members of his family to work in corporate America, and one of the first African American managers in his company. He was acutely aware of the family's expectation that he would not only survive, but that he would thrive within the corporation. In some respects it was more daunting than the expectations of his superiors. Although he could talk to family members about his trials and tribulations, he was reluctant to do so. Early in his life, Bill would have shared his troubles with his brothers, sisters, and best friend. They would have helped him blow off steam as they offered a reality check about his reactions and solutions. But Bill had abandoned that source of support when he became a corporate success.

Although he still perceived his daily surroundings to be hostile and unsupportive, he no longer felt free to talk to his extended family about this. He had become the family's great success story. To confess that he was still troubled by racial indignities felt too much like an admission of failure. He was afraid that such an acknowledgment would serve to discourage those of his relatives with less education. If *he* could not succeed, with all of his education and opportunities, what could *they* expect out of life? Most of all he was ashamed to reveal that he was no longer as outspoken and confrontational as his family traditions had taught him to be. He had become overly cautious about how he appeared to others. The pressure to succeed had transformed him into a conformist, despite a strong family legacy emphasizing self-respect and honor above all else. In the face of this conflict, he found no role models or mentors he could turn to in the business world. But Bill knew he could not grovel or whine about his circumstance in perpetuity. His family training required him to do something about it—something that in the end would still elevate his stature.

After the urging of another African American coworker and confidant who did not have the family supports Bill had, and who thought he was crazy for not using them, he got up enough courage to share his troubles with his older sister. It was she who had always helped him to disclose his troubles to the family, and she was his buffer against sharp criticisms. It was she who helped Bill to understand that other family members had experiences that were similar to Bill's and that their insights could be of some help—if he could get past feeling embarrassed by what he saw as failure.

Lesson Number Five: Be Clear about Your Dream

The experiences of an African American man in American society can easily make race his preoccupation.

At some point every African American man, directly or indirectly, encounters attitudes and beliefs that reflect the racism designated specifically for him. So long as this country continues to use discrimination and prejudice to limit full participation and acceptance of people of African descent, no person who looks like, or can be identified as an African American will be free of the uneven treatment reserved for us. Consequently, crafting a world view and a self-image that employs a positive African American identity becomes an important counterweight to the negativity heaped on us.

The importance of this comes through recognizing how the invisibility syndrome works to undermine belief in self and how the need to "be somebody" without an identity that is linked to a vision with a clear purpose will set you up as a tool of whatever circumstance you find yourself in, conveniently boxed in by stereotypes.

Claudine, an old film staring James Earl Jones and Diahann Carroll, has a scene in which some of this conflict is illustrated. Jones's character is a garbageman courting Diahann Carroll, a single mom on welfare with several children. One day, while visiting the family, an unexpected visit from the caseworker creates chaos in the apartment, as everyone scurries to hide luxury items and any other prohibited signs of income—including Jones, who is forced into a closet out of the sight of the caseworker. When this charade falls apart, Jones indignantly informs the caseworker that he is employed, doesn't apologize for what he does, has no responsibility for the family, and shouldn't be put in such a position by his courtship of the mother. Many black men and women identified with that movie scene.

With the many assumptions about them existing in various contexts, black males who are uncertain of their identity become more prone to fill what roles are wanted by others, erroneously believing that what others offer is what we actually want. It is a seduction that suggests a fulfillment of the insatiable human need for acceptance. African American men who are not clear about their dream or identity can be doomed to wander into situation after situation that demand our accepting an inappropriate image in exchange for belonging. For some of us, the need to be included and to be approved by others can be so great that it forces us to sacrifice our identity and dream. Who are we, if we are not who we are?

Lesson Number Six: Beware of the Victim Mentality Trap

By this point, you've seen many times that experiences of racism have created a propensity among some African American men to embrace a "victim's mentality." Since there is considerable testimony among us on discrimination and ample evidence of overt injustices, it is easy for black men to use racism as an excuse for their personal shortcomings. Self-empowerment, however, requires a realistic appraisal of our circumstances, in order to identify when racism is at fault or when we are at fault for our own inability to achieve personal goals. Here are two examples of this lesson in action:

One evening when talking with friends Harry went on and on, in a tirade about how he is likely to get laid off at his job. He was upset about losing the income, and he thought he was being treated unfairly by his employers. "They always fire us first," was Harry's assessment of his circumstances. His friends tried to comfort Harry by going over the details of his situation. They knew Harry had a tendency to be late and was difficult to get along with, and the impression of many employers was that he was overqualified for the positions he applied for. It was well-known among his friends that Harry had been drifting for years, uncertain of what he wanted to do. He seemed to be, by his behavior, not interested in much more than *talking* about making money, and satisfied with just getting by.

For five years Mason had been a reporter for a local newspaper in a small city. He was one of two black employees at the paper. The other person was a female secretary. For years Mason had asked for different assignments, beyond reporting on activities in the black community, and crime, which was most of his work. On the one hand he had responded to this job for the expressed purpose of the paper's need to improve their coverage of the African American community. On the other hand he saw himself becoming typecast as the black reporter for the black community. Mason felt he was falling into a professional rut that would do little for his career. When he approached his bosses with his observations they denied any malicious intent and gave him what they considered several plum assignments, like covering the Reverend Jesse Jackson's speech and fundraising dinner for the Democratic Party when he came to town.

Both Harry and Mason have job circumstances that can easily place blame on either of the parties for the situation. Harry felt like a victim, when clearly many of his friends saw Harry's drifting as the problem. Mason felt like a victim also, and, in fact, was told by others before he took the job that the local newspaper had a bad record of supporting the careers of any of its employees of color. Mason is more likely a victim of racism than Harry is, but there is enough ambiguity in the details for uncertainty to prevail in either case. Furthermore, when we all engage in self-evaluations of our own decision making in career choices there is always room for second-guessing ourselves, which makes identifying acts of racism difficult.

Lesson Number Seven: Know What You Can and Cannot Change

Another tool for self-empowerment is learning to distinguish what you can change from what you cannot. This is vital, since many African American men spend considerable time and energy fighting their own view of racism, even figments of their imagination. We struggle with inner conflicts when it may be unnecessary. As a mentor once said to me, "Learn how to pick your battles, consider strategic retreats, and keep your eyes on the prize." This is not the easiest task when one is frequently provoked by acts of prejudice and discrimination—acts that stir within us that masculine urge to strike back. But the wisdom of knowing what you can and cannot change, along with wisely picking your battles, makes you discover that not every battle is worth fighting, because not every racial slight is worth responding to.

It is difficult to be so wise when your self-respect is under attack. Your judgment gets entangled in the inability to step back, think clearly, reassess, renew, and find alternatives. Sometimes you do have to accept the current hand dealt to you, until such time as you are dealt a better one. But you still keep looking for those opportunities that will change your life for the better, and you still try to create better opportunities in your life through unquestionable performance. This is reflected in the movie *Glory,* a powerful film about the 54th Massachusetts Infantry, an all-black unit of the Union Army during the Civil War. Although risking their lives for the cause, they were still seen as slaves, unpredictable in their allegiance and thought by many to be unable to make a significant contribution to the war effort. But this regiment fought valiantly, suffering a great loss of life in the battle to free Fort Wagner from the Confederate Army. The Tuskegee airmen, along with other black soldiers in World War II, also struggled with suspicions about their allegiance and doubts of their ability, causing the army brass to give them restricted roles in the fighting.

Kevin played by the rules to become eligible to take the New York Police Department's sergeants exam. It was a tortuous path for him, navigating through the police bureaucracy and departmental favoritism. After finally gaining the privilege to take the exam, he failed, later learning that his failure would have an impact on the perception of African American candidates. Kevin believed that his performance would discourage other eligible African American officers from taking the test, as well as give some supervisors more personal reasons not to encourage promising candidates. He was furious, but was uncertain what to do next. He sought advice from me and every other person or organization that would help him pass the test or file a grievance.

The ability to know what you can and cannot change is the ability to gain a fresh perspective—an ability to not read the same old meaning into the same old story of racial encounters. For black men, this becomes a crucial aspect of sustaining energy and keeping the focus on self-empowerment. It really requires knowing yourself.

Lesson Number Eight: Beware of Personal Gremlins

Our internal barriers are *our* creations. I like to call them our "personal gremlins." They reside inside our heads, our guts, our hearts, and our souls. They are the thoughts and emotions that stop us cold and prevent us from doing the things we say we want to do. You know—those mind games and head trips we put ourselves through, particularly when we get indignant. Some of us use our chronic indignation from racial slights to cover up our own insecurities, like challenges to go head-to-head with white males on the job, or to say no to our addictions to alcohol, drugs, or women.

Lesson Number Nine: Assemble Supports

An extremely important feature in learning about self-empowerment is finding the support in friends, relatives, colleagues, or professionals that will appropriately validate life experiences, and will facilitate positive energizing of empowerment initiatives. Having these supports in one's life helps to maintain personal sanity. We must *appropriately* validate our life experiences, because simply being surrounded by "yes men" to uphold our view of our experiences may only contribute to an unreal outlook, leading to immobilizing frustrations. Having friends or family join you in wallowing in self-pity quickly moves beyond the constructive need for validation and toward crippling despondency and depression. We need to have people who can provide a balanced view around us when we're making decisions.

Lesson Number Ten: Dream

A well-developed plan is an essential part of achieving change and accomplishing goals: it is empowerment. However, many of us approach new initiatives, in spite of thorough and thoughtful plans, with nagging skepticism or cynicism about the likelihood of success. Our caution grows out of witnessing others struggle with the limits on black male success. Many black men believe that we are held back, rather than supported, in our efforts to attain a better life.

Smitty is a twenty-eight-year-old African American man who worked for five years at an auto repair shop fixing flats, repairing tires, doing alignments, and replacing brakes. He sees no future in this work as an employee, but is interested in opening his own shop. In the past months he has visited several locations that he believes could serve as a good place to do business. His wife, Marie, is fearful and discouraging of this risky venture. She reminds him of his responsibilities to his children and frets over his leaving a good job. Part of her concern comes from warnings emanating from her circle of friends and family who have had loved ones pursue "bright ideas," only to see disappointment crush their spirit and change their relationship.

Smitty's confidence was built on the knowledge that he is an excellent tire and brake repairman, one who is often consulted by his boss as well as by other workers. "He knows his stuff," was the comment offered by his boss, customers, and coworkers. By working closely with his boss, Smitty had also learned something about the business of running a repair shop.

When Smitty tried to get a business loan he ran into redlining. He found the banks unwilling to approve a loan for start-up costs, although he had his savings and his car as collateral. When he tried leasing property, he encountered delays from uncooperative and inaccessible landlords, or excessive demands for up-front security money.

His job was in jeopardy because of a decline in his performance, in turn due to his preoccupation with the details of trying to start his own business. Ultimately, Smitty shelved the idea, because of the deleterious effects it was having at work and at home.

In his heart Smitty believed that his lack of success was in part due to white bank loan officers who looked at him and thought, "This black man is not capable of running his own business." In addition, he was convinced that many of the landlords he contacted had the same thoughts—that he would "run out on the lease." Smitty agonized over whether white attitudes prevented his success, or if it was due to his not being completely prepared for these attitudes. Was there something he could have done to dispel these notions before they came up? It wasn't as if he was stupid and didn't anticipate these types of racist doubts about his ability. Smitty's questioning of his own preparation was the beginning of an anguishing period of, "Was it me, or was it them?" Later, his wife, family, and friends would fervently take one or the other position in trying to convince him that the outcome wasn't a personal tragedy. But Smitty found little comfort in their efforts. He saw their goodwill as shot through with their own ambivalence and conflicts about what a black man could and could not do in this country.

A history of these kinds of circumstances, coupled with the inability to distinguish when it is racism or individual effort, can be so distorting and injurious to the person's self-esteem that he can be driven to embrace solely simplistic explanations, such as "blaming the system," as a means of preserving his sanity and achieving some emotional stability.

Lesson Number Eleven: Risk Change

Despair in African American men about the efforts we must exert ("you must be twice as good in order to get half as much") breeds an ingrained pessimism about success in the white man's world, and arrogance about choices we do make. Given this attitude, we must have courage to take risks in self-empowerment that are likely to bring us face to face with racism. This means what I call "going up to the edge," that is, pushing yourself beyond personal doubts and going after what you want, taking risks in pursuit of your vision. It means exerting control over your belief in yourself. It means being able to go down into the valley of your own insecurities, confident you can conquer any emotional risks because of the way you have thought through your plan and gained faith in yourself. It means not tossing in the towel when the going gets tough. It means understanding the virtue of sacrifice today for tomorrow's benefit.

When I first met Terry I told him he was an alcoholic. He denied it. His girlfriend said he lies, and she claims that he has several beers for lunch on the job and more when he comes home each night, plus a joint. His response is that at least he does not drink hard liquor any more. I got Terry into recovery for several years of fighting the addiction. During his recovery his girlfriend left him, he lost old friends, and he moved from job to job. Terry suffered from chronic indignation, seeing racism in every situation he encountered. It frustrated him and was a reason he drank. He kept at his recovery, at understanding and controlling his indignation, at doing better on the job; he also kept struggling with an unspoken desire to become a minister. Afraid of humiliation by his friends' discovery, Terry felt unworthy of this career. However, encouraged over the years of his recovery by Alcoholics Anonymous—as well as by counseling, spiritual guidance from his pastor, support from new friends, and returning to school—Terry ultimately became a minister and community organizer. It was a ten-year journey.

Lesson Number Twelve: Find Your Spiritual Anchor

As African American men, we must reconnect to, or attain for ourselves, a deep abiding belief in an inner personal spirit, divine or otherwise, that provides us with an unswerving faith and confidence in ourselves, our worthiness, and the righteousness of our personal vision and goals. I tremble to mention the word "divine," because some of us black men have developed a negative view of what the church and organized religion have done to spirituality, as well as of their failure to remedy the difficulties in our community. More pointedly, many African American men see the black church as catering more to the soul or egos of church leaders, and thus failing in offering the leadership we need to change the realities of our lives. But this sentiment too often covers an unspoken need that many of us have for a spiritual connection and inner optimism about our destiny. In disregarding the church and organized religion, we have thrown the baby out with the bathwater.

To overcome the barriers of racism, the disillusionment of invisibility, we must have a spiritual center, an inner faith and optimism that will sustain us through difficult times. A family friend, Dr. Samuel De-Witt Proctor, the late senior pastor of the Abyssinian Baptist Church in Harlem, once proudly showed me his chronicle of the generations of successful Proctors from the Tidewater, Virginia, area. Many were first in their careers and exhibited considerable determination along with a strong family spiritual grounding in achieving their success. The title of his book, *Substance of Things Hoped For,* was taken from a passage of bible scripture that has been his guide throughout life. Taken from Hebrews, chapter 11, verse 1: *Now faith is the substance of things hoped for, the evidence of things not seen.* The older I get, the more apparent is the wisdom in that scripture.

On some level we must attain a sense of destiny, a gut-level feeling that our efforts lead toward fulfillment of our vision and goals. We must feel that something greater than the particular steps in our plan also enact our personal visions, that destiny is also guided by faith, or feelings deep in our souls—not just what we have thought through. It is this spiritual anchor that has allowed so many African Americans to succeed when others have decreed our failure.

11

Strategies for Moving On

It was good hearing from Bill after the support group had ended. He had left New York City for work in a small corporation in the south, where he'd received a promotion and more opportunity to advance professionally. When he called me, it was to invite me to join him and all of the former group members for dinner on an evening when he was planning to be back in town. He wanted to test out his idea of starting a network of support groups for African American men, starting with his church and national fraternity.

I was surprised and impressed to learn that he had already begun the process. He had contacted a few of the group members already, as well as his family members. His leadership and proposal for the network had inspired the backing of a major foundation.

"Legacy, Doc, remember? It's all about sharing our legacy."

Bill's emphasis on legacy reminded me of his prior resistance to family stories about coping and making it through life. I thought of how he struggled to live up to them. Now he had adopted this as a major strategy for a mentoring program. He had become his brother's keeper, partnering with potential helpers as an emissary of new values about black manhood: reducing personal guardedness, lessening interpersonal tension, and elevating mutual cooperation.

Bill had become less self-absorbed and more giving and sharing. He wanted other men like him to come to terms with how much getting over, slipping and sliding, or being slick really harmed them. He understood that, to heal from invisibility, our standards have to be serious, purposeful, and sacred.

Coming Together as Men and Brothers

We have seen that there can be a huge psychological gap between African American men over closely held values and beliefs about those things we consider important and necessary—such as the way we talk, dress, walk, or present ourselves as African American. The invisibility syndrome exploits our differences and our conflicts over racial identity. Our hunger to be accepted and our uncertainties about being black and of African descent leads us down many different identity paths with little general agreement, except this: the inner drive to survive and thrive, coming closer to the vision we grasp of manhood.

Finding our way to visibility and acceptance is a major theme in our lives as African American men. Showing the side we want people to see is not uncommon for people to do from time to time. Our being manipulative and fluid with our image—often behind the facade of being "cool" behind our multiple masks—is a survival technique. It is necessary for survival, but a barrier to working together on a common agenda. We can be difficult to figure out. We know this about each other and can become equally skeptical and clandestine about our intents. We give up little information about who we are. Getting to know each other can be hard. Because getting beyond our personal screens and filters means dropping defenses honed often over a lifetime, our conversations can be both superficial and validating at the same time. But intimate conversation between black men is worth encouraging; in fact, it can be transforming.

How to Start a Discussion or Support Group

Coming together for purposeful conversation can happen in many ways. In fact, it does not require any special arrangements if we use what already exists—the places we currently meet. It is not where we meet that's important, it is what we do when we meet. It is helpful and illuminating to talk in groups of ten or twelve, but even when it is only two of us the tasks are:

- to find a way to work with each other, communicate real trust in each other, and be at ease with one another
- to talk to each other honestly and discover like-mindedness, while respecting differences of opinion
- to find means of cooperation that benefits other African Americans
- to rise above pettiness and self-indulging behavior
- to return black male leadership to the community through healthy partnerships with African American women
- to take responsibility for what you can do for yourself to reduce the symptoms of invisibility

The best way to organize a discussion group is by inviting those men with whom you already have some level of trust. You must enter into a pact together, an agreement that says that above all, you will be honest with each other and honor each other's disclosures. An initial step must include addressing any tensions that exist between you, as well as discussing what you understand to be the tensions in black male relationships in general.

Before you ask any further questions that may reveal true thoughts and feelings, start with both the simplest and at the same time most difficult thing—looking at each other. Permitting open and honest conversation without the risk of exploitation or putdowns means fighting temptation—the habit of one-upmanship and our inclination for gaining advantage of one another.

Asking Probing Questions

Contrary to popular belief, the underlying purpose of asking questions is not always to get hard and fast answers. Questions serve many purposes: to create opportunities to share information and seek validation; to listen and be heard; to comfort and find comfort; to discover and explore differences; and to find common ground—these are just a few. Here are some questions to begin with in a group, or by yourself.

You don't need a group to unmask invisibility. Begin by locating your own stories about being an invisible man. The following questions will help bring those memories to the surface:

- Have you frequently felt that your behavior was misinterpreted because of what people assumed about you?
- Have you been in conversations and felt that no one responded to your comments?
- Have you frequently had your answer to a question dismissed, only to have the same answer accepted from someone else?
- Have you ever stood at a counter waiting, only to be overlooked by the clerk or salesperson?
- When was the last time you asked yourself, "How come no one sees me?" What happened?

These questions resonate for most of us. They tend to provoke the gesturing-to-the-chest, finger-pointing anger I almost invariably hear in the life stories of black men, and they open up views that may be blazing in their candor or acute in their painfulness, even though the experiences may be decades old.

On the other hand, there are many questions you can ask yourself and others that also clarify feelings and values by prompting heart-warming, inspiring memories, such as:

- Who were your role models as a child?
- Who do you really admire in the world today?
- Who helped convince you to not quit or give up on your life?
- Who stuck by you?
- Who encouraged you to get an education?

Use any or all of these questions as a starting point.

Suggestions and Advice for Black Men

Here are guidelines that might also help you start to resolve fundamental issues with invisibility on your own and with others.

1. Have a personal vision or dream, then come up with a realistic plan to get it.

Never let the minefield of indignities and preconceptions about black men make you shut down. Set short- and long-term life goals. Think positively! Believe in the possible. Believe in yourself.

2. Work on your mind, how you view things and your visibility.

Attitude can be everything! You *are* somebody! Find the courage to fight off any negative things people say and do to make you invisible, the "dream snuffers." Dr. Joseph White, a black elder and friend, followed his mother's wisdom, "Make something out of nothing," make things happen in your life. From the wisdom of another black male elder: "Eliminate *can't* from your vocabulary." You must believe you can conquer your inner demons. Learn to compensate for your weaknesses and capitalize on your strengths.

3. Fight for your education.

Stay in school or go back to school. It's never too late to get an education. Learn a skill, advance yourself to the next professional level. Become visible on *your* terms. Get teachers to help you. Have parents or friends help you. Talk to others about your dream and enlist them to help you. Create a team of life and workplace coaches. Pull together a plan and implement it. Reevaluate your relationship to those who do not fully support your vision to better yourself. Learn to recognize good help and advice. Be flexible and open to suggestions.

4. Fight for your right to work and advance in your career.

Map out your career and where you want to go through advancement. Go get the appropriate knowledge and skills. Don't be afraid to leave one job and seek another if you were made invisible, humiliated, and ashamed of what you did or became. You find the job that fits, that makes you visible in the workplace. Consult elders with work experience for advice. Find a mentor. Mobilize!

5. Read about successful black people; talk to those who model success.

Work twice as hard to get what you want, not what you can't get. Be clear about the visibility you can achieve and be focused in its attainment. Identify black men who have been successful and go talk to them. Ask around, have others give you names to help you find persons. Talk to black male elders and your peers who have a positive outlook. Seek those with success in their relationships with family, jobs, and good friends. Look among the ordinary folks, as well as among those with notoriety. Find them! They are there, they're just invisible.

6. Learn to make and keep commitments, and be responsible.

"Actions speak louder than words." When you strive for visibility, if you can't keep a promise, don't make it. You must be definite and clear about your intentions. Make a commitment to change in ways you always wanted to. Make it to yourself, to your partner, to your family, to your career, and to your life. Then back it up by doing what you say. You must be consistent and dependable in this behavior. It's how true you are to your word. Visibility is a matter of integrity: toward yourself and others.

7. Be a father to your children.

Our children are expressions of our visibility. They are our legacy. Make a commitment to be a part of your children's life. Be there for all of them, most certainly some of them, but never none of them. Create your own special time with them. Work out communications problems with mothers, for the sake of the children. Read books on black parenting, such as *Boys Into Men: Raising Our African American Teenage Sons* by Dr. Nancy Boyd-Franklin and Dr. A. J. Franklin. Talk with friends and peers who are having success as fathers. Establish a fathers' group. Have a fathers' outing with your buddies. Include grandfathers, or other black male relatives and elders, into activities with your children.

Helping Helpers Help

At the end of my all-day workshops I am surrounded. Counselors, psychologists, social workers, ministers, and other participants want to speak with me individually. They are not blind to the invisibility experienced by black men, but they express long-standing feelings of helplessness to change things.

"How can I do better in my work with black men?" they ask. This is a legitimate question. Many of my white colleagues, especially, realize that their race or gender is a barrier that makes it difficult for many black men to connect with them successfully. Some people admit confidentially that racism in their private attitudes and beliefs gets in the way. Others suspect that their organization or agency has problems that hinder effective work with black men. I get requests to help participants deal with policies and practices that put black men in a bind.

My answers to these diverse post-workshop inquiries tend to fall into four general categories:

1. Look at what you already do effectively.
2. Examine your own personal awareness of the way you act.
3. Consider ways to help your profession and organization to be more responsive.
4. Enlighten others by sharing information and by example.

Look at What You Already Do Effectively

To helpers I say, look first at ways you are already working or have worked effectively with black men. Many of you have some awareness and level of understanding about issues discussed in this book. If invisibility is a central theme in the lives of black men—a perspective I consider a very useful way to understand men of African descent and their experiences in society—it can be a lens to help you, as well, to reexamine your practices and personal relationships with them.

Your capacity to empathize—not sympathize or patronize—has, perhaps, given you cherished moments of genuine connection to the discontents and joys of black men. Recall the way you were during these times. Identify what you did, and the appropriate attitude, behavior, and temperament you displayed. I tell participants, don't throw out what you know works for you, build on it. Appreciate how your ability to connect to people in general can be utilized to further your potential to talk with men of African descent. Having an open line of communication with black men gives you the opportunity to grow in practical knowledge and wisdom about our view of the world. More importantly, you'll open up opportunities to enlist us into partnerships toward resolving some of our difficult issues. Sometimes that's as easy as saying these simple words, "What do you think?" or, "How would you handle this situation?"

I remember working with Jim's apprehensions about his son's direction, and his passion to be a good father figure. He was relieved when I enlisted his ideas about how he thought I could best help his son. Several times we talked through mutual parenting strategies, blending my professional insights with his conventional wisdom about family life, being a provider, and challenges living in his community. Jim didn't feel put down or snubbed, in spite of my credentials or expertise, but rather complemented, as we pursued a mutual goal—the welfare of his son. It is very important to not overlook what black men do well.

Examine Your Personal Knowledge and Behavior

Another request I make of persons genuinely wanting to reach out and connect with black men is to engage in self-examination. I ask people, How much do you know of African American history? There are those who look at me a little befuddled, with raised eyebrows, as if to say, "What does that have to do with techniques to help black men?" I tell them how important the historical background of our treatment in the United States is to their working effectively with men of African descent. The way we all see things has been shaped by history, and there is no dismissing it as a framework for the codes of the brotherhood.

So, I advise my inquiring colleagues to read John Hope Franklin's classic black history primer, *From Slavery to Freedom.* Or, to read James Jones's most readable and scholarly masterpiece, *Prejudice and Racism.* I encourage them to read the thoughts of many black authors on the black male experience in Herb Boyd and Robert Allen's anthology, *Brotherman.* The number of scholarly and literary works abound from a rich pool of authors, such as Ralph Ellison, Richard Wright, James Baldwin, Cornel West, Michael Eric Dyson, Zora Neale Hurston, Toni Morrison, Dorothy West, Alice Walker, Angela Davis, bell hooks, Maya Angelou. And these are just a few. There is abundant and diverse literature representing the history and life experiences of people of African descent. In other words, I say, make some time to be a student and read about our history, culture, and arts. There is a reading list at the end of this chapter.

I also ask those huddled around me during these precious moments of workshop debriefing to look at their own behavior toward black men. This is a serious request for self-examination. I recommend they verify with others how they come across when around black men. There are so many other situations when we ask for feedback (for example, on our work, appearance, athleticism), why not for this purpose also? Our finely tuned detectors for racism as men of African descent indicate that serious self-monitoring by others is necessary. Students of human behavior know that the way we act and treat each other determines the course of our interpersonal relationships. Therefore, elevating individual personal knowledge and awareness of our own behavior among men of African descent can contribute to effectiveness as professionals and as human beings.

Consider Ways to Help Your Profession and Organization to Be More Responsive

What I consider as a very positive outcome from my workshops is that people tell me they return to their workplace motivated to make their services more responsive to men of African descent. I charge participants to go back and raise two key questions:

- "How do black men, women, and families view our agency's services and overall role in their lives?"
- "How does our agency provide the resources, support, and quality care needed and desired by the African American community?"

I also recommend at least three ways to begin this undertaking:

1. *Share the information from the workshop.*

I encourage participants in my workshop to share with their coworkers what they have learned and gained from attending my workshop; help them to become more aware of their attitudes, and beliefs about black men; make copies of my handouts and give them to coworkers; show, by example and information, how their interpersonal interactions with black men have changed; set aside time for special staff meetings to discuss these issues.

2. *Encourage coworkers' self-examination of their professional and personal interactions with black men and women.*

I urge returning participants to find ways to foster self-examination among their coworkers. Look at their professional practices and personal ways they interact with black men and women. My recommendation is to make this part of their staff development training. Use the notions of personal power behind the invisibility syndrome as a template to scrutinize conventional wisdom and practices that have become so entrenched in the way we professionally and personally work with and relate to black men.

3. *Review program and policies of the organization to determine any complicity with the creation of invisibility for African Americans.*

Many of our institutional practices are held hostage by our agency's and government's regulations. Nevertheless, it does not mean we cannot be more adept at implementing them more fairly, and perhaps flexibly. Within many of our individual work responsibilities we have the latitude to be more flexible and compassionate in interpreting and applying the rules. Most of us know how to work within the rules governing our jobs. We should be public advocates for change of social policies and practices that are exclusionary, disenfranchising, or impede the personal development of black men.

Enlighten Others by Sharing Information and by Example

A final challenge that I raise in my chat with people is to make a personal investment in enlightening others in their various social networks—not only coworkers, but friends and family. I ask participants to help friends, neighbors, and relatives to understand how invisibility hurts, by utilizing their own experiences for the sake of enlightenment. This may be the most important gain from our day-long work together. Thoughtful people recognize that this knowledge is not exclusively for professionals, and should not be compartmentalized in such manner. I ask, for example, "What do you do in response to hearing stereotype thinking and biased attitudes? Do you speak up and provide alternative knowledge?"

How people behave in those situations where they hear or see misrepresentation and maligning of men of African descent, or any other persons or groups for that matter, is the key to long-range change in public and private attitudes.

My Advice on Personal Relationships

A number of people are interested in discussing their private and personal relationships with men of African descent. There are those who have intimate attachments, such as family, husbands, partners, sons, or close friends. And some of these relationships are in trouble. Some people want to intervene before they become more of a problem. Some people are simply curious about the psychology of the black man they are close to. In other words, they want to learn why he behaves the way he does.

For those who have serious relationship issues—such as marital troubles or parental problems, such as a son's truancy and acting-out behavior—I advise a therapist or appropriate professional. It is my experience that too often we, as black men and women, wait until problems reach almost crisis level before seeking professional assistance. Often it is very late to resolve issues at those points, since conditions have become chronic and more resistant to interventions.

For people who want to understand better the black men they are close to, I advise sharing what they have learned at the workshop. I tell them to talk with husbands or sons about what they learned. Discuss some of the major points with a best friend or relative. Learn if they experienced invisibility in the manner I represented, or have they experienced it differently, if at all.

What is contained in this book can make for wonderful conversation, debates, and the exploration of worldviews. Through that process alone we are brought closer together, and perhaps to greater understanding of each other.

Suggestions and Advice for Black Women

Black women participating in my workshops are often passionate in expressing their frustrations. They identify as their own many of the issues I cover. Black women also have an extraordinary invisibility of their own. But it is not only about being a professional or a coworker with black men that concerns them. It's how much of my workshop touches upon their personal relationships with husbands, partners, fathers, sons, brothers, or male friends. To black women, I say:

1. Whenever you get a chance, talk with your elders and learn from their views about black men.

First, go to the elder you have the closest relationship to—father, mother, uncle, aunt, minister, or neighbor. Consider dropping in on a senior center. There are many black seniors who would love to share their stories and wisdom. Ask seniors how they managed relationships with the black men in their lives. What did they learn from their fathers, brothers, uncles, husbands, or from any other intimate relationships they care to share. Share your special concerns. Don't worry if the elder person's views reflect a different time or generation. Look beyond age. Seek the wisdom from it.

2. Find black male role models.

If you are raising children, particularly male children, make a deliberate effort to find a black male role model. If possible, find more than one, since diversity broadens experiences and wisdom. Let relatives be your first choice, if they meet your criteria and values. Then look within your circle of friends. Inquire within organizations you are affiliated with, such as the church, community centers, or even at work. Role models are frequently around us in the form of ordinary people. Be open to possibilities, such as coworkers, neighbors, or even a brother or friend of a friend. At all times be clear about your standards and careful in determining who has access to your family, your children, and your personal life.

3. Talk with other women who have had any type of meaningful relationship with a black man.

With this suggestion I include daughters with fathers, sisters with brothers, or women who are good neighbors, or in a positive coworker relationship with black men. Of course, find those who have had enduring intimate relationships as marital partners or lovers. There *are* couples that have had lasting marriages. Find out how they handled the ups and downs of an enduring relationship. The goal is to tap into their insights. What was at the source of their bond?

4. Read books and view videos about black men in search of manhood.

Visit a bookstore or library and pick up some books or videos that give a history of blacks in America. Use existing archives of media, with the purpose of broadening your understanding of the black experience. Look particularly to comprehend the challenges for both black men and women. Chart our progress in classic documentaries, such as *Eyes on the Prize* or Web sites, such as The Black World Today (*www.tbwt.com*). Watch movies, such as *Malcolm X,* as well as the series *Roots,* found in video stores—fact-based docudramas that can be used to engage interests and discussions. Seek out librarians, friends, teachers, or anyone else who can guide your research. Form a group of sisters who are willing to have discussions with you. Make it a social activity or black history club. Better yet, find like-minded black men to join you.

5. Make this book a discussion topic by giving it to others and setting up discussion groups.

Give a copy of this book to your husband, partner, father, or other male acquaintances. Talk with them about the topics I discuss in the book. Do they agree or disagree with the points and experiences in the book? Ask, What have been their experiences; how similar are they to the examples in the book; what did they do; how do they cope; what's their philosophy on living and surviving as a black man?

Also use the book with your girlfriends. See how much you and they agree or disagree with the issues, examples, and explanations. What have you learned and what more do you need to learn about black men? In other words, make conversation with the book.

6. Things to consider as a mother:

Help your son discuss his experiences of invisibility in school. Talk to him, using the examples in the book, to find out if he has had these experiences.

Read to your son and daughter at an early age from children's books on African American history. Exposure to the resilience of African Americans in our history is another way to lay the foundation for a strong self-esteem, life purpose, and clear identity. In other words, help them find interest in the lives of successful people of African descent, demonstrated in biographies and other living examples.

Nurture the development of a positive identity by exposure to people and the places that appropriately represent your values. Spend some time at the places where your child acquires life experiences about visibility.

Talk to your children about being of African descent, what it has meant to you, and what it has meant to previous generations—the members of your family. You can do this by outlining the family tree and talking about family members, their views, experiences, and philosophy of life. How are their views of the world similar or different from yours and how did they acquire them? Did their generation make a difference? What were their dreams and relationships, and are there better ways to do things?

7. As a wife or partner: Learn how to defuse anger and rekindle the flame of love.

When conversations with your partner turn into a power and control struggle (perhaps personified by a shouting match) no one wins, so find a way to call a time out, a cooling off period— this is handling anger by defusing the situation. For example, calmly suggest that you both talk about it later with cooler heads. Resist the temptation to be more provocative. Wait until he has calmed down. Both of you are responsible for making this happen. Don't get into verbal or physical abuse.

When you do talk again, be prepared to do a lot of listening. In fact, listen first. Remember that a black man's visibility in the relationship is essential for an intimate partnership. If the issue is his visibility in the home and with his children, ask how he wants to be seen as father and partner. Draw out his practical and concrete thinking about these roles.

Don't cut him off at first disagreement. Remember, your objective is to try to listen first and find out what's important to him.

Then negotiate! We all have different beliefs about how we want to be, and they change with age and circumstances. Be honest with each other about your beliefs now. Recognize that they may have changed since you first met.

If the issue is your love life, rekindle the flame. Remember the things you did together during courtship. Resurrect those activities you both enjoyed then, or find new ones appropriate for now. Make time to spend together. Date again and make time for love. Make your home a refuge for both of you.

Rediscover what you both like as leisure activities and do them. Reengaging and maintaining a relationship sometimes requires going along with activities your partner is more interested in than you are. Find a way to share time, if not activities.

Be a visible support in his work efforts and career pursuits, too. Recognize his accomplishments, no matter how small. Be a source of encouragement. Help him plan his career and think through his options. Help him talk about and figure out the best way to handle the little indignities at work.

The more you become a consistent source of psychological support, the more likely your partner will be to become mobilized in solving his problems. And, the more likely he will become the provider and supporter you've always desired.

8. Don't be afraid to seek professional help through counseling.

Through professional counseling you can work on your couple relationship and deal with the impact of invisibility upon your family. If you can't get your man to go with you as a couple at first, go yourself for some individual consultations and professional guidance to gain some clarity and to determine how best to engage your partner in the counseling process.

Suggestions and Advice for Professional Colleagues

1. Advance your knowledge of the invisibility experience by reading the history of African Americans.

Consider all non-fiction and fiction works about African Americans. Look up African American Web sites. Talk with African American friends or acquaintances for recommendations. Visit with librarians for guidance. Visit or consult with the local university's black or ethnic studies departments for information. Most have Web sites. Locate the professors who are experts. Inquire at black bookstores.

2. Examine your own behavior and attitudes toward black men.

Recognize and eliminate patterns in your behavior that make black men invisible. Talk about the examples in the book to friends or others to assess your attitudes and behavior. Are there African American friends or acquaintances you can engage in discussion about issues in the book? Help others in your network of peers, family, and friends to do the same.

3. Have training workshops on the invisibility syndrome in your school or workplace.

Lobby for training support from upper management. Propose workshops and discussion groups on the invisibility of black males in the workplace. Advocate for the training of colleagues and staff about policies and workplace practices related to these issues. Target supervisors and your workforce. Campaign for degree programs in your field to formalize training in service delivery issues to African Americans. Encourage special attention to the challenges and needs of black men. Contact your national organization for information and guidance. Inquire locally to find other professionals, organizations, or agencies with the best practices. Pool your knowledge and resources to work together, for example, in sponsoring workshop training and bringing in experts.

4. For counselors, psychologists, social workers, psychiatrists

Consult each of your national associations for information and resources on ethnic minority issues. Health disparities are a chronic manifestation of invisibility. Go to the U.S. Department of Health and Human Services, Office of Minority Health for reports (*www.hrsa.gov/omh/*). In your workplace, establish black men's groups to discuss invisibility, their survival as black men, and ways to be resilient facing these challenges. Find organizations locally working with black men, and collaborate—form partnerships to address these issues and learn of the best practices to arrive at remedies.

5. For Ministers

Establish and develop a men's ministry. Make this book the focus of discussions. Extract areas from the book to guide interventions, such as father groups, couple relationships, or men's fellowship. Create black men's groups, or a place for them to discuss invisibility, survival, and life dreams. Encourage support groups for them. In individual, couples, or family pastoral counseling, assist members in understanding the ramifications of invisibility to their relationships. Have training and focused discussions on the invisibility syndrome and black male issues in your regular minister meetings, regional conferences, and annual national conventions. Educate your fellow ministers on these issues. Bring it into your seminary curriculum, particularly for training in pastoral counseling.

6. For Teachers

Examine your classroom practices and your teaching techniques to determine if they promote black male invisibility. How do black boys and men feel treated in your class, such as being recognized, answering questions, getting tutored? Ask your students about their experience in your class. Talk to those black students you have a relationship with. Talk to fellow teachers about their insights and suggestions. Seek out and weigh different opinions.

Be aware of how classmates and other peers represent and treat black males in school. Address negative attitudes toward black boys in the class. Listen to the concerns of black parents. Talk to those black parents you have a relationship with. Raise concerns about invisibility syndrome at the next Parent Association meeting. Use this book!

Advocate with administration and colleagues for more information and resources in working with the invisibility of black male students. Ask for teacher training on these issues. Bring in experts.

Tell the Story: Encouraging the Values of Manhood

Think about the stories you've read in this book. Think about your own. Think about the black men you know. Do you see the connections? Can you imagine tapping that knowledge and using it to help someone—perhaps yourself—step out of the invisibility trap? Tell the story, especially to our youth. Teach and encourage these values:

- Responsibility
- Commitment
- Knowledge of self
- Knowledge of history of peoples of African descent
- Being able to trust each other
- Sharing
- Confidence
- Belief in self
- Defying spirit
- Spiritual beliefs
- Education
- Competence
- Provider
- Protector
- Compassion
- Intimacy
- Leadership

A few years ago, on a warm Mississippi afternoon, I had the opportunity to discuss my thinking about invisibility and visibility with faculty and students at Jackson State University. Beaming proudly in the front row in his Sunday-go-to-church finest was my oldest cousin,

Cleveland, who lived nearby. An elder of my family, he had shared my father's childhood. So, it was as important to me to have him in the audience as it was for him to be there.

Afterwards I wondered whether my academic presentation made sense to Cleveland. So, as we drove home, I asked him.

"I believe I do," he said in his rich Mississippi drawl. Then he launched into one of his trademark stories:

"When I was a young boy on Mama's farm, I wandered one morning over to our pond and saw some ducklings swimming around. So I started skipping stones 'cross the surface of the water. The ducks all rushed up on the other side of the pond to get away from me, all but one. That little thing kept swimming around in circles going nowhere fast, kicking the water up something furious. It seemed the more he tried, the more he got nowhere. So I waded out into the pond to that little duckling and picked him up."

Cleveland made a quick scooping motion with his hands, lifting them in the air.

"I discovered a turtle had that duck by his foot, holding on real tight under that water where I could not see him. That's what stopped that little duckling from getting up on land to join the others." Cleveland looked at me to be sure I was ready for his point. "That's like what you mean by your invisibility thing. Like that turtle out of sight under the water. There are things that we can't see or know in a person's life that can grab onto him and hold him back. Keep him from getting on land when he needs to."

I looked at Cleveland in awe for few moments.

"You got it," I said, marveling at the simple wisdom of elders.

SUGGESTED READINGS

Benston, K. W., ed. *Speaking for You: The Vision of Ralph Ellison.* Washington, D.C.: Howard University Press, 1990.

Billingsley, A. *Climbing Jacob's Ladder: The Enduring Legacy of African American Families.* New York: Simon & Schuster, 1992.

Boyd, H., and Allen, R. L., eds. *Brotherman: The Odyssey of Black Men in America.* New York: Ballantine Books, 1995.

Boyd-Franklin, N., and Franklin, A. J. *Boys into Men: Raising Our African American Teenage Sons.* New York: Plume, 2000.

Boyd-Franklin, N. *Black Families in Therapy: Understanding the African American Experience.* 2nd ed. New York: Guilford Publishers, 2003.

Branch, T. *Parting the Waters: America in the King Years 1954–63.* New York: Simon and Schuster, 1988.

Chatters, L. "Religion and Health: Public Health Research and Practice." *Annual Review of Public Health,* 21 (2000): 335–367.

Chiplin, C. K. *Roads from the Bottom: A Survival Journal for America's Black Community.* Brandon, Mo.: Quail Ridge Press, 1996.

Clarke, R. M. *Family life and school achievement: Why poor black children succeed or fail.* Chicago: University of Chicago Press, 1983.

Cose, E. *The Rage of a Privileged Class.* New York: Harper Collins Publishers, 1993.

Cross, W. E. *Shades of Black: Diversity in African American Identity.* Philadelphia: Temple University Press, 1991.

Duneier, M. *Slim's Table: Race, Respectability, and Masculinity.* Chicago: The University of Chicago Press, 1992.

Dyson, M. E. *Reflecting Black: African American Cultural Criticism.* Minneapolis: University of Minnesota Press, 1993.

Edwards, A., and Polite, C. K. *Children of the Dream: The Psychology of Black Success.* New York: Doubleday, 1992.

Essed, P. *Understanding Everyday Racism: An Interdisciplinary Theory.* Newbury Park, Calif.: Sage Publications, 1991.

Feagin, J. R., and Sikes, M. P. *Living with Racism: The Black Middle-class Experience.* Boston, Mass.: Beacon Press, 1994.

Franklin, A. J. "Friendship issues between African American men in a therapeutic support group." *Journal of African American Men,* 3(1) (Summer 1997): 29–43.

Franklin, A. J. "The invisibility syndrome." *The Family Therapy Networker,* 17(4) (July/August 1993): 32–39.

Franklin, A. J. "Invisibility syndrome and racial identity development in psychotherapy and counseling African American men." *The Counseling Psychologist,* 27(6) (November 1999): 761–793.

Franklin, A. J. "Therapeutic support groups for African American men. In *African American Males: A Practice Guide,* edited by L. E. Davis. Thousand Oaks, Calif.: Sage Publications, 1999.

Franklin, A. J. "Therapy with African American men." *Families in Society: The Journal of Contemporary Human Services* (Summer 1997): 350–355.

Franklin, A. J. "Treating anger in a support group for African American men." In *New Psychotherapy for Men: Case Studies,* edited by W. S. Pollack and R. F. Levant. 239–258. New York: John Wiley & Sons, 1998.

Franklin, A. J. "Visibility is important too: Viewing the larger systemic model." *The Counseling Psychologist,* 27(6) (November 1999): 820–826.

Franklin, A. J., and Boyd-Franklin, N. "Invisibility Syndrome: A clinical model towards understanding the effects of racism upon African American males." *American Journal of Orthopsychiatry,* 70(1) (January 2000): 33–41.

Franklin, A. J., and Davis, T. "Therapeutic support groups as a primary intervention for issues of fatherhood with African American men." In *Clinical and Educational Interventions with Fathers,* edited by J. Fagan and A. J. Hawkins, 45–66. Binghamton, N.Y.: The Haworth Press, 2001.

Franklin, J. H., and Moss, A. A. *From Slavery to Freedom: A History of African Americans.* 7th ed. New York: Alfred A. Knopf, 1994.

Gordon, E. T., Gordon, E. W., and Nembhard, J. G. "Social science literature concerning African American men." *Journal of Negro Education,* 63(4) (1995): 508–531.

Graham, L. O. *Our kind of people: Inside America's black upper class.* New York: HarperCollins Publishers, 1999.

Grier, W. H., and Cobbs, P. M. *Black Rage.* New York: Basic Books, Inc., 1968.

Hammond, R., and Yung, B. "Psychology's role in the public health response to assaultive violence among young African American men." *American Psychologist,* 48(2) (1993): 142–154.

Jackson, J., Chatters, L., and Taylor, R. *Aging in Black America.* Newbury Park, Calif.: Sage Publications, Inc., 1993.

Jackson, J., Chatters, L., and Taylor, R. *Family Life in Black America.* Newbury Park, Calif.: Sage Publications, Inc., 1997.

Jaynes, G. D., and Williams, R., eds. *A Common Destiny: Blacks and American Society.* Washington, D.C.: National Academy Press, 1989.

Johnson, E. H. *Brothers on the Mend: Understanding and Healing Anger for African American Men and Women.* New York: Pocket Books, 1998.

Jones, J. M. *Prejudice and Racism.* 2nd ed. New York: McGraw-Hill, 1997.

Kitwana, B. *The Hip Hop Generation: Young Blacks and the Crisis in African American Culture.* New York: Basic Civitas Books, 2002.

Lazur, R. F., and Majors, R. "Men of color: Ethnocultural variations of male gender role strain." In *A New Psychology of Men,* edited by R. F. Levant and W. S. Pollack, 337–358. New York: Basic Books, 1995.

Leary, W. E. "Discrimination may affect risk of high blood pressure in Blacks." *The New York Times,* (October 24, 1996): A20.

Madhubuti, H. *Black Men: Obsolete, Single, Dangerous? The Afrikan American Family in Transition.* Chicago: Third World Press, 1990.

Majors, R., and Billson, J. M. *Cool Pose: The Dilemmas of Black Manhood in America.* New York: Lexington Books, 1992.

McCall, N. *Makes Me Wanna Holler: A Young Black Man in America.* New York: Random House, 1994.

McIntosh, P. "White Privilege: Unpacking the Invisible Knapsack." *Independent School,* (Winter 1990): 31–36.

Mental Health: Culture, Race, and Ethnicity: A Supplement to Mental Health: A Report of the Surgeon General. Rockville, Md.: U.S. Public Health Service, 2001.

Miller, J. G. *Search and Destroy: African American Males in the Criminal Justice System.* New York: Cambridge University Press, 1996.

Monroe, S., and Goldman, P. *Brothers: Black and Poor—A True Story of Courage and Survival.* New York: Ballantine Books, 1988.

Neighbors, H., and Jackson, J. *Mental Health in Black America.* Newbury Park, Calif. Sage Publications, Inc., 1996.

Neighbors, H., and Williams, D. "The epidemiology of mental disorder among African Americans: 1985–2000." In *Health Issues in the Black Community,* edited by R. Braithwaite and S. Taylor. San Francisco: Jossey-Bass, Inc., 2000.

Pleck, J. H. "The gender role strain paradigm: An update." In *A New Psychology of Men,* edited by R. F. Levant and W. S. Pollack, 11–32. New York: Basic Books, 1995.

Powell, K. *Step into a World: A Global Anthology of the New Black Literature.* New York: John Wiley & Sons, Inc., 2000.

Proctor, S. D. *Substance of Things Hoped For.* New York: G. P. Putnam's Sons, 1996.

Ridley, C. R. "Clinical treatment of the nondisclosing Black client: A therapeutic paradox." *American Psychologist,* 39(11) (November 1984): 1234–1244.

Riggs, M., producer and director. *Ethnic Notions.* (Available from California Newsreel, 149 Ninth Street/420, San Francisco, CA 94103), 1987. Videocassette.

Riggs, M., and Kleinman, V., producers, and Riggs, M., director. *Color Adjustment.* (Available from California Newsreel, 149 Ninth Street/420, San Francisco, CA 94103), 1991. Videocassette.

Sexton, A., ed. *Rap on Rap: Straight-up Talk on Hip-hop Culture.* New York: Delta, 1995.

Staples, R., and Johnson, L. B. *Black Families at the Crossroads: Challenges and Prospects.* San Francisco: Jossey-Bass Publishers, 1993.

Steele, C. M. "A threat in the air: How stereotypes shape intellectual identity and performance." *American Psychologist,* 52(6) (June 1997): 613–629.

Steele, C. M., and Aronson, J. "Stereotype threat and the intellectual test performance of African Americans." *Journal of Personality and Social Psychology,* 69 (1995): 797–811.

Sutton, A. "African American men in group therapy." In *Men in groups,* edited by M. P. Andronico, 131–150. Washington, D.C.: American Psychological Association, 1996.

Taylor, R. L., ed. *African American Youth: Their Social and Economic Status in the United States.* Westport, Conn.: Praeger, 1995.

Tucker, B. T., and Mitchell-Kernan, C., eds. *The decline in marriage among African Americans.* New York: Russell Sage Foundation, 1995.

Vanzant, I. *The Spirit of a Man: A Vision of Transformation for Black Men and the Women Who Love Them.* New York: HarperSanFrancisco, 1996.

West, C. *Race Matters.* New York: Vintage Books, 1993.

White, J., and Cones III, J. *Black Man Emerging: Facing the Past and Seizing a Future in America.* New York: Routledge, 1999.

Wideman, D. J., and Preston, R. B. *Soulfires: Young Black Men on Love and Violence.* New York: Penguin Books, 1996.

Wright, J. A. Jr. ed. *From one brother to another: Voices of African American Men* vol. 2. Valley Forge, Penn.: Judson Press, 2003.

Wright, J. Jr. *Good News: Sermons of Hope for Today's Families.* Valley Forge, Penn.: Judson Press, 1995.

Wyatt, G. E. *Stolen Women: Reclaiming Our Sexuality, Taking Back Our Lives.* New York: John Wiley & Sons, Inc., 1997.

ADDITIONAL READINGS

Akbar, N. *Visions for Black Men.* Nashville, Tenn.: Wilson-Derek Publishers, Inc., 1991.

Anderson, E. A. *Streetwise: Race, Class and Change in an Urban Community.* Chicago: The University of Chicago Press, 1990.

Anderson, N. B., ed. "Behavioral and sociocultural perspectives on ethnicity and health," [Special issue]. *Health Psychology,* 14(7), 1995.

Bell, D. *Faces at the Bottom of the Well: The Permanence of Racism.* New York: Basic Books, 1992.

Belton, D., ed. *Speak My Name: Black Men on Masculinity and the American Dream.* Boston, Mass.: Beacon Press, 1995.

Bogle, D. *Toms, Coons, Mulattoes, Mammies, and Bucks: An Interpretive History of Blacks in American Films.* 3rd ed. New York: Continuum Publishing, 1994.

Bowman, P. J. "Coping with provider role strain: Adaptive cultural resources among Black husband-fathers." In *African American Psychology: Theory, research, and practice,* edited by A. K. H. Burlew, W. C. Banks, H. P. McAdoo, and D. A. Azibo, 135–151. Newbury Park, Calif.: Sage Publications, 1992.

Bowser, B. P., and Hunt, R. G., eds. *Impacts of Racism on White Americans.* 2nd ed. Thousand Oaks, Calif.: Sage Publications, 1996.

Boyd, H., ed. *Autobiography of a People: Three Centuries of African American History Told by Those Who Lived It.* New York: Doubleday, 2000.

Boyd-Franklin, N., and Franklin, A. J. "African American couples in therapy." In *Revisioning family therapy,* edited by M. McGoldrick, 268–281. New York: The Guilford Press, 1998.

Calamari, J. E., Cox, W. M., and Roth, J. D. "Group treatments for men with alcohol problems." In *Men in groups: Insights, interventions, and psychoeducational work,* edited by M. P. Andronico, 305–321. Washington, D.C.: American Psychological Association, 1996.

Carter, R. T. *The Influence of Race and Racial Identity in Psychotherapy.* New York: John Wiley & Sons, 1995.

DeLa Cancela, V. "'Coolin': The Psychosocial Communication of African and Latino Men." In *African American males: A critical link in the African American family,* edited by D. J. Jones, 33–44. New Brunswick, New Jersey: Transaction Publishers, 1994.

DuBois, W. E. B. *The Souls of Black Folk.* Chicago: A. C. McClurg and Company, 1903.

Franklin, A. J. "The Invisibility Syndrome in Psychotherapy with African American Males." In *African American Mental Health,* edited by R. L. Jones. Hampton, Va.: Cobb and Henry Publishers, 1998.

Frazier, E. F. *Black bourgeoisie.* New York: Free Press, 1957.

Hacker, A. *Two Nations: Black and White, Separate, Hostile, Unequal.* New York: Charles Scribner's Sons, 1992.

Hecht, M. L., Collier, M. J., and Ribeau, S. A. *African American Communication: Ethnic Identity and Cultural Interpretation.* Newbury Park, Calif.: Sage, 1993.

Hillard III, A. G. *The Maroon Within Us: Selected Essays on African American Community Socialization.* Maryland: DuForcelf published by Black Classic Press, P.O. Box 13414, Baltimore, MD 21203-3414, 1995.

Hooks, B. *Yearning: Race, Gender, and Cultural Politics.* Boston: South End Press, 1990.

Hopson, D. S., and Hopson, D. P. *Friends, Lovers, and Soulmates: A Guide to Better Relationships Between Black Men and Women.* New York: Simon & Schuster, 1994.

Hutchinson, E. O. *The Assassination of the Black Male Image.* Los Angeles: Middle Passage Press, 1994.

Jones, A. C. *Wade in the Water: The wisdom of the spirituals.* Maryknoll, New York: Orbis Books, 1993.

Jones, R. ed. *Black Psychology.* 4th ed. Hampton, Va.: Cobb Henry Publishers, in press.

July II, W. *Brothers, Lust, and Love: Thoughts on Manhood, Sex, and Romance.* New York: Doubleday, 1998.

Karenga, M. *Kwanzaa: A Celebration of Family, Community and Culture.* Los Angeles: University of Sankore Press, 2560 West 54th Street, Los Angeles, CA 90043; (323) 205-9799, 1985.

Kunjufu, J. *Countering the Conspiracy to Destroy Black Boys: Vol. I.* Chicago: African American Images, 1983.

Levine, L. W. *Black Culture and Black Consciousness: Afro-American Folk Thought from Slavery to Freedom.* New York: Oxford University Press, 1980.

Liebow, E. *Tally's Corner: A Study of Negro Streetcorner Men.* Boston: Little, Brown, 1967.

Lincoln, C. E., and Mamiya, L. H. *The Black Church in the African American Experience.* Durham, No. Car.: Duke University Press, 1990.

Oliver, W. *The Violent Social World of Black Men.* New York: Lexington Books, 1994.

Parham, T. A. *Psychological Storms: The African American Struggle for Identity.* Chicago: African American Images, 1993.

Pasick, R. S. "Friendship Between Men." In *Men in Therapy: The Challenge of Change,* edited by R. J. Meth and R. S. Pasick, 108–127. New York: The Guilford Press, 1990.

Pollack, W. *Real Boys: Rescuing Our Sons From the Myths of Boyhood.* New York: Random House, 1998.

Tarpley, N., ed. *Testimony: Young African Americans on Self-Discovery and Black Identity.* Boston: Beacon Press, 1995.

Taylor, R., Mattis, J., and Chatters, L. "Subjective religiosity among African Americans: A synthesis of five national samples." *Journal of Black Psychology,* 25 (1999): 524–543.

Terkel, S. *Race: How Blacks and Whites Think and Feel About the American Obsession.* New York: Anchor Books, 1992.

Tobias, R. A. *Nurturing At-Risk Youth in Math and Science: Curriculum and Teaching Considerations.* Bloomington, Ind.: National Educational Service, 1992.

Watts, R. J., and Jagers, R. J., eds. *Manhood Development in Urban African American Communities.* New York: The Haworth Press, Inc., 1997.

Wideman, J. E. *Fatheralong: A Meditation on Fathers and Sons, Race and Society.* New York: Pantheon Books, 1994.

Willis, A. C., ed. *Faith of Our Fathers: African American Men Reflect on Fatherhood.* New York: Dutton, 1996.

Yalom, I. D. *The Theory and Practice of Group Psychotherapy.* 3rd ed. New York: Basic Books, 1985.

APPENDIX

BLACK MEN: FACTS AND FIGURES

The total African American population in the United States, based on the U.S. Census, 2000, is 12.9% of the United States population. This includes those (6%) that reported being black as well as one or more other races. Whites make up 77.1% of the U.S. population. Black males make up 6.1%, and black females make up 6.8% of the total U.S. population. From 1990 to 2000 the black population grew by 21.5%, in comparison to 13.2% growth in the total population.

Of the total black population, 47.5% are males, and 52.5% are females. Blacks under the age of 18 make up 32.5% of the total black population, 18–64 are 59.6%, and 65 years and over, 7.9%.

About 53.6% of the African American population lives in the south, 18.8% in the midwest, 18% in the northeast, and 9.6% in the west.

In a 1999 Census report, 23.3% of black men (white men, 12.3%) had less than high school education; 37.8% of black men (white men, 32.1%) were high school graduates; 24. 7% of black men had some college (white men, 25%); and 14.2% of black men (white men, 30.6%) had a bachelor's degree or more.

In the 1999 Census report, black men (17%) are less likely to be employed in managerial and professional jobs than white men (32%). Twenty percent of black and white men were employed in technical sales and administrative support occupations. White men (19%), more likely than black men (14%), were in precision production, craft, and repair jobs. Seventeen percent of black men (white men, 8%) were in service occupations, 31% of black men (white men, 17%) were operators, fabricators, and laborers.

Median wage and salary income (year 2000 dollars) for black males is $25,177, and for females is $19,953. Twenty two percent of the black population meets the poverty status criteria, in contrast to 7.5% of whites who are below the poverty line. Thirty percent of blacks under eighteen are below the poverty line.

In the 1999 Census Report, 47% of all black families were married couple families, 45% were maintained by women with no spouse present, and 8% percent were maintained by black men with no spouse present. In 1998, 28% of all black families and 52% of all white families had incomes of $50,000 or more. Twenty-three percent of black married couple families (white married couple families, 33%) reported an income of at least $75,000. Sixty-seven percent of black families maintained by women with no spouse present (whites, 33%) had incomes less than $25,000.

Age-adjusted mortality rates for selected causes of death per 100,000 population in the U.S. in 1998 (the latest year for which data are available): heart disease: (whites, 123.6; blacks, 188.0); stroke: (whites, 23.3; blacks, 42.5); lung cancer: (whites, 38.3, blacks, 46.0); female breast cancer: (whites, 18.7, blacks, 26.1); homicide: (whites, 3.2, blacks, 26.1). Black men die from prostrate cancer at three times the rate of white men and are twice as likely to die from diabetes.

An estimated 12% of black males in their twenties and early thirties were in state or federal prison or local jails in 2001.* Thirteen percent of black males age 25–29 were in prison or jail, compared to 4.1% of Hispanic males and about 1.8% of white males in the same age group. Black males make up 44.6% of the total number of male inmates in state and federal prisons or local jails (as of June 30, 2001), compared to 38% white male inmates, or 15.7% hispanic male inmates.

---

*"Prison and Jail Inmates at Midyear 2001," Bureau of Justice Statistics Bulletin, U.S. Department of Justice, Office of Justice Programs, April 2002, NCJ 191702.

U.S. Census Bureau Web Site

www.census.gov/population/
www.socdemo/race.html.

INDEX